Questions and Answers
KNOWLEDGE

The **What**, **When**, **Where**, **How**, and **Why**
of everything you need to know

Author: Louise Spilsbury
Consultants: Tony Sizer, John Williams, David
Lambert, Simon Adams, Mandy Holloway,
Steve Parker
This edition produced by Tall Tree Ltd,
London
First published by Parragon in 2007

Parragon
Queen Street House
4 Queen Street
Bath BA1 1HE, UK

ISBN 978-1-4054-9460-1

Printed in China

Questions and Answers
KNOWLEDGE

HOW? WHY? WHERE? WHEN?

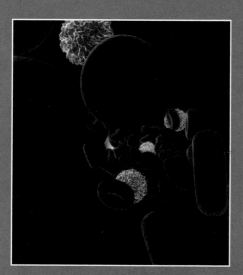

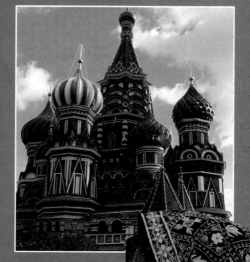

Louise Spilsbury

CONTENTS

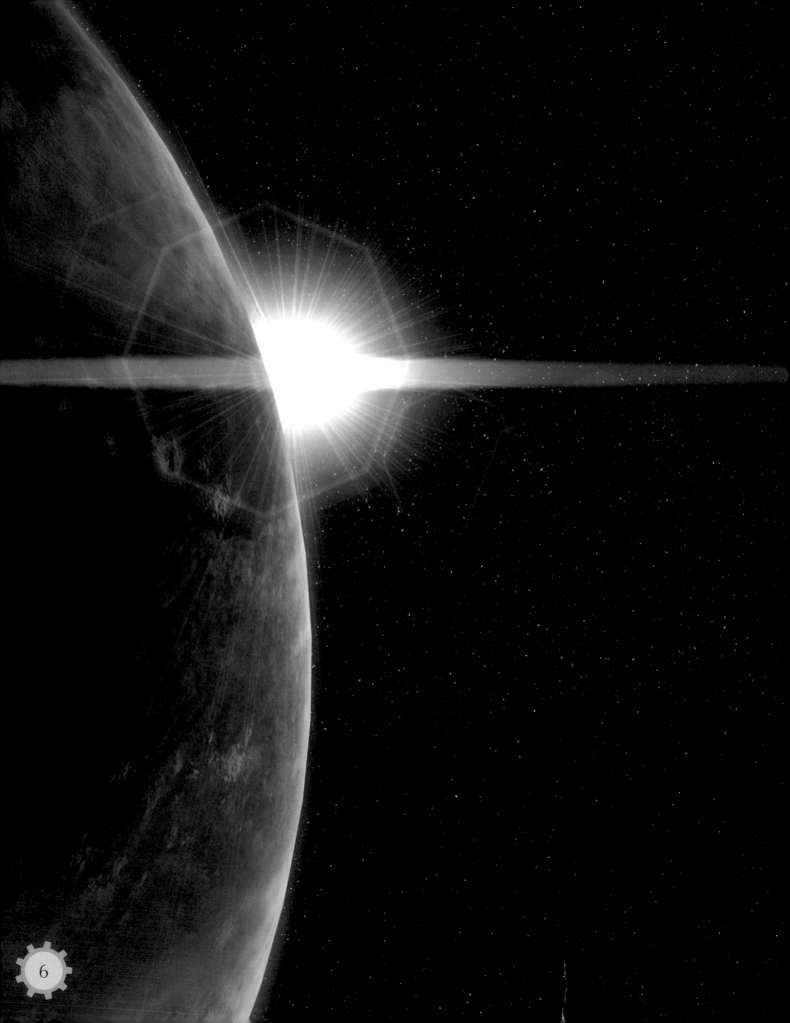

EARTH AND SPACE

Earth is one of a group of planets that orbits the enormous ball of burning gas that is the Sun. Although you might think that Earth is huge, it is only a tiny speck when compared with the vast size of the universe, with its billions of stars and galaxies. On its surface, Earth is a restless, changing planet, with erupting volcanoes, shaking earthquakes, and powerful forces that are continuously changing the landscape.

THE BIG BANG

What was the Big Bang?

The Big Bang was an explosion that created the whole universe. About 14 billion years ago, the universe exploded outward from a hot, dense bubble that was smaller than a pinhead. The universe quickly grew larger than a galaxy and kept on expanding. As it slowly cooled, tiny particles (pieces) within it joined and began to form the stars and planets.

The Big Bang exploded from a tiny point called a singularity.

BELOW Stars begin as clouds of gas like this, called nebulae.

When did the first stars shine?

The first stars began to shine about 300 million years after the Big Bang. Particles began to clump together and formed clouds of gas. These slowly grew and became hotter and hotter. Eventually, the center of these clouds became so hot that the clouds exploded and became the balls of fire we call stars. New stars are born and die every day.

BELOW There are about 200 billion stars in the Milky Way galaxy.

DID YOU KNOW?
Some of the stars we can see in the night sky are so far away that the light coming from them has taken millions of years to reach Earth.

How many galaxies are there?

There are more than 100 billion galaxies in the universe. A galaxy is a large group of stars, dust, gas, rocks, and planets. Most stars in the universe are found in galaxies. The Sun and planet Earth are part of our galaxy, the Milky Way. Astronomers have photographed many galaxies through special telescopes. With the naked eye, people can only see three galaxies beyond the Milky Way.

A telescope uses glass lenses to magnify distant objects.

Is the universe changing?

Yes, the universe is still growing and expanding today. Some scientists believe that the universe will keep expanding. Others think that the expansion will start to slow and eventually stop. They believe that the universe will then start to shrink until it crunches together into a tiny space and sparks off another Big Bang.

9

THE SUN

What is the Sun?

The Sun is just an ordinary star, one of billions of stars in the universe. The Sun has a special name and is important to us because it is close enough to give Earth light and warmth. This light and warmth is what allows plants, animals, and other living things to survive on our planet. Without the Sun there would be no life on Earth.

Close-up pictures of the Sun show the hot gases gushing out from its surface.

BELOW Solar panels like these trap some of the Sun's energy and change it into electricity we can use. The word solar means "having to do with the Sun."

How Hot is the Sun?

The temperature at the core, or center, of the Sun is about 29 million degrees Fahrenheit. From the core, this incredible heat energy flows to the surface, where the temperature is closer to 11,000 degrees Fahrenheit. This is still so incredibly hot that it would melt anything it touched.

the Sun so bright?

The Sun is the brightest object in the sky because it is a giant ball of brightly glowing gas. Light from the Sun takes just over eight minutes to reach Earth, but when it gets here it is still so powerful that its light can damage your eyesight. That is why you should never look at the Sun directly and always wear sunglasses on sunny days.

DID YOU KNOW?
The Sun is about five billion years old and it is more than 600,000 miles wide. It is so big that more than one million Earths could fit inside it.

Solar eclipse
seen here

MOON

EARTH

SUN

ABOVE The Sun is about 400 times wider than the Moon. However, because the Moon is about 400 times closer to Earth than the Sun, both the Moon and the Sun look about the same size in the sky from Earth.

solar eclipses happen?

The Moon travels around Earth. A solar eclipse happens when the Moon comes between the Sun and the Earth and casts a huge shadow onto the Earth. A total eclipse is rare, but when it happens, the Sun seems to disappear from the sky and for a few moments everything becomes cold and dark.

THE SOLAR SYSTEM

JUPITER

SATURN

VENUS
EARTH
MARS

SUN

MERCURY

What is the solar system?

The solar system consists of the Sun and the planets that move around the Sun in oval paths called orbits. A planet is a vast ball of rock or gas that travels in orbit around a star. There are other objects in our solar system, too, such as moons and asteroids.

DID YOU KNOW?
The Sun is so far away that if you tried to drive there, traveling at 60 miles an hour, it would take you 170 years to reach your destination!

How far are we from the Sun?

Earth is 93 million miles away from the Sun. This means that our planet is far enough away from the Sun for water to be liquid. If Earth were closer and, therefore, warmer, water would turn to gas, and if it were farther away, water would become ice. It is Earth's distance from the Sun that makes it the only planet in the solar system that is known to support life.

URANUS

NEPTUNE

PLUTO

These are the nine planets of our solar system. Earth is the third planet from the Sun.

Why do planets orbit the Sun?

The planets move around the Sun because the Sun is so big that its gravity is very powerful. Gravity is the force that pulls the planets toward the Sun. It is strong enough to hold all the planets in the solar system in their orbits, moving around the Sun in the same direction.

When did Earth form?

Earth and the other planets formed about five billion years ago. Our planet was born from dust and gases whirling in orbit around the Sun as it was forming. In the intense heat, the dust and gases collided and hardened into a ball of rock. Even today, the Earth is still hit by dust from space and the occasional large piece of rock.

13

THE ROCKY PLANETS

Which are the rocky planets?

Mercury, Venus, Earth, and Mars are known as the rocky planets because they are mainly made of rock and metal. Mercury is closest to the Sun. Although it is burning hot on this planet during the day, at night it becomes freezing cold. This is because Mercury's atmosphere is very thin and there are no clouds to trap and hold warmth during the night.

We cannot see the surface of Venus because it is always covered in thick clouds.

MERCURY

VENUS

Which is the hottest planet?

Although Venus is the second planet from the Sun, it has the hottest surface. It is hotter than Mercury because it has a blanket of fast-moving clouds around it. This traps heat from the Sun and stops the heat flowing out into space. The thick atmosphere on Venus is mostly made up of carbon dioxide gas, which would be deadly poisonous for people.

Earth called the blue planet?

Earth is often called the blue planet, because three-quarters of its surface is covered in water and from space it looks blue. When the Earth formed, a layer of gas formed around it. This layer protects the Earth from getting too hot or too cold. Eventually, rain began to fall and formed our planet's rivers, lakes, and oceans.

DID YOU KNOW?
Some scientists believe there could be life on Mars. Although it is too cold for life to exist on the surface, tiny organisms could exist in warmer pockets below the ground.

EARTH

MARS

What makes Mars red?

Mars is known as the red planet because of the color of its soil. The surface of Mars is rich in iron oxide, which is rust and has a reddish color. Mars has little atmosphere and gets very cold. Like Earth, it has ice caps on its north pole and south pole but the rest of its surface is a dusty red desert.

THE GAS PLANETS

What are the gas planets?

Jupiter, Saturn, Uranus, and Neptune are known as the gas planets. These planets are large spinning balls of gas with small rocky cores (centers). Jupiter and Saturn are also known as the giant planets because they are so big. Jupiter is twice as heavy as all the other planets put together and Saturn is almost as large as Jupiter.

Jupiter is the largest planet in the solar system. The bright colors you can see are formed by the different gases in Jupiter's clouds.

BELOW Saturn's famous rings orbit around its middle. The rings are very thin compared to the size of the planet, none being more than 165 feet deep.

Why does Saturn have rings?

Saturn's rings are made up of dust and pieces of rock, and ice. Astronomers think that the dust and rock may have come from moons that broke up when they crashed into other objects in space. The millions of chunks of ice-covered rock that form the colorful rings are held in orbit around Saturn by the pull of the planet's gravity.

HOW many moons does Jupiter have?

Jupiter has 63 moons, and possibly more. A moon is an object that orbits around a planet. Some moons are rocky and round, but they can be icy or volcanic. Jupiter also has rings, like Saturn, but they are smaller and fainter. Uranus and Neptune have rings, too.

ABOVE If you look at Jupiter with binoculars, you can easily see its four main moons. Italian astronomer Galileo Galilei was the first person to see these moons, along with Saturn's rings, in 1610, using an early telescope.

DID YOU KNOW?

Some of the billions of pieces of dust, rock, and ice that make up Saturn's rings are as big as a house. Others are as small as grains of sand.

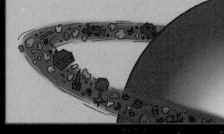

URANUS

PLUTO

When were Uranus, Neptune, and Pluto discovered?

Astronomers discovered Uranus, Neptune, and Pluto later than the other planets because these planets are so far away. Uranus was found in 1781, Neptune in 1846, and Pluto, which is five times smaller than Earth, in 1930. Pluto is so small that astronomers argue it is not a planet at all. It is also so far away that no maps have yet been made of its surface.

NEPTUNE

ASTEROIDS, COMETS, AND METEORS

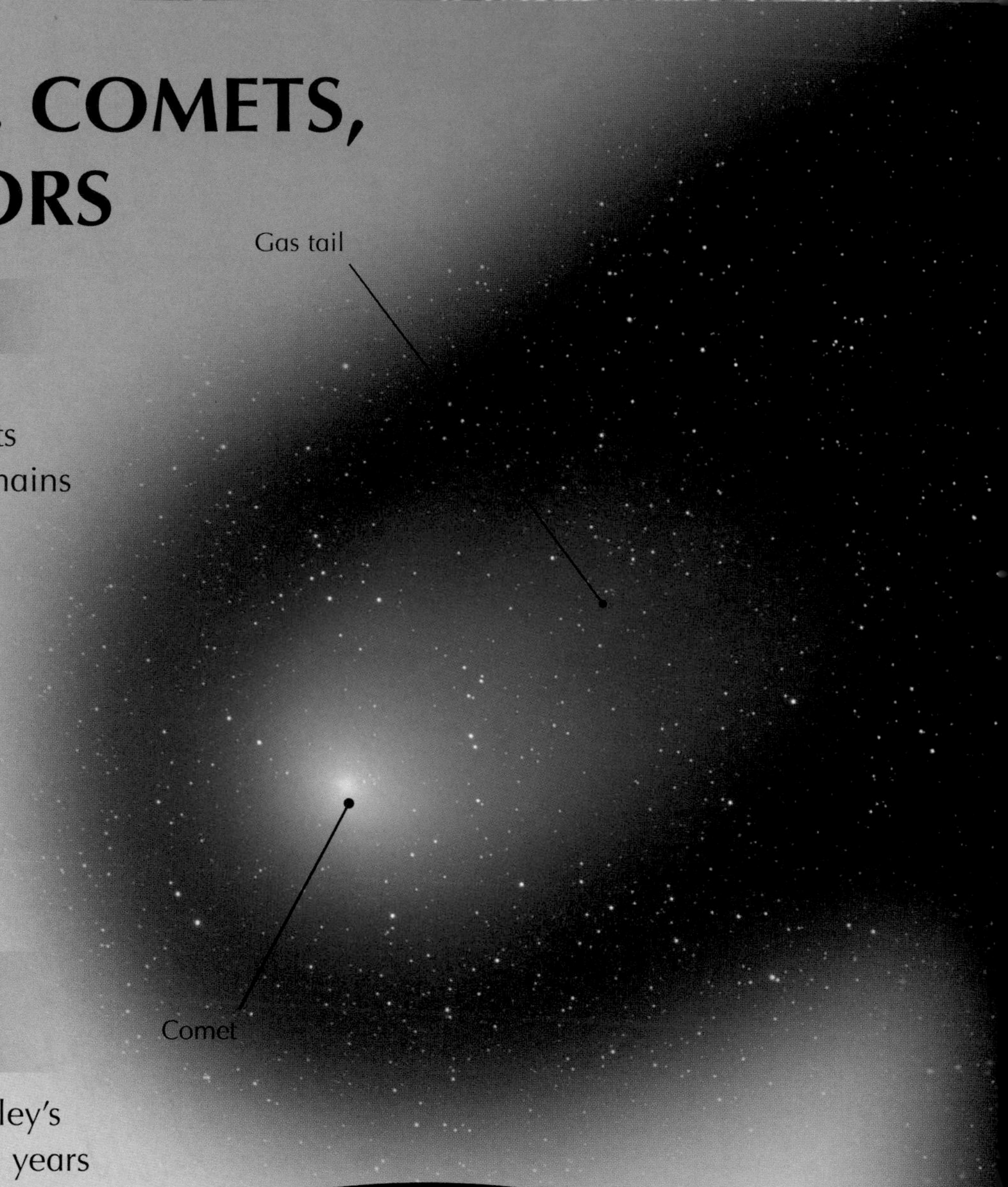

What is a comet?

A comet is a lump of rock, ice, and frozen gas that orbits around the Sun. A comet remains icy and frozen while its orbit carries it far from the Sun. When it gets closer to the Sun, the frozen gas and dust evaporate and form a glowing tail that can stretch for millions of miles.

Gas tail

Comet

When can we see Halley's Comet?

The most famous comet, Halley's Comet, can be seen every 76 years and will reappear in 2061. People have been observing this comet for more than 2000 years. It was named after English astronomer Edmond Halley, who, in 1682, realized the comet had been seen before. About 20 different comets can be seen from Earth each year.

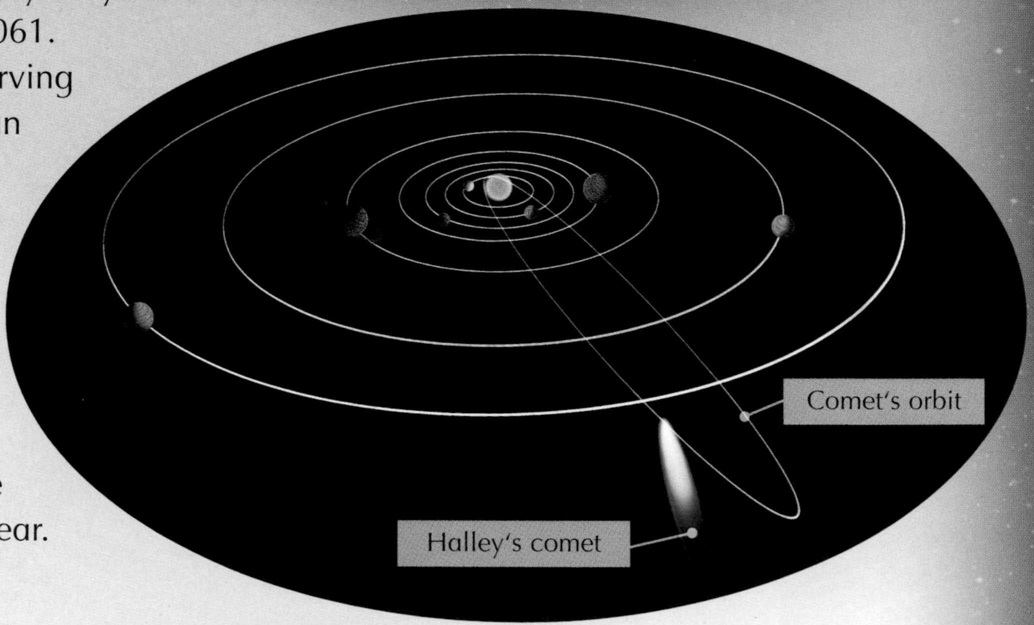

Comet's orbit

Halley's comet

HOW big is an asteroid?

Asteroids are oddly shaped rocks that travel in orbit around the Sun. They range in size from tiny particles to huge lumps nearly 600 miles across. Most asteroids are found in what is known as the Asteroid Belt, between Mars and Jupiter. Others travel in an orbit closer to the Sun. Some have been pulled into the orbits of planets, such as Jupiter, Mars, and Earth, by these planets' gravity.

Where do meteorites come from?

Meteorites are pieces of rock that come from outer space. When they reach Earth, they usually burn up in the atmosphere, where they can be seen as as streaks of light called meteors. The few that make it through Earth's atmosphere and hit the surface are meteorites. Most are the size of pebbles, but, long ago, huge meteorites made vast craters in Earth's surface.

THE MOON

How big is the Moon?

The Moon is about a quarter of the size of Earth and measures 2,160 miles wide. The Moon is Earth's only natural satellite and is held in orbit by the pull of Earth's gravity. It takes the Moon about four weeks to complete one orbit of the Earth. Our word "month," which means a period of about four weeks, comes from the word "Moon."

BELOW Scientists believe that there are large amounts of frozen water hidden in craters on the Moon's surface. A crater appears as a dark shadow on the Moon's surface.

Crater

Sea

Why is the Moon covered in craters?

The Moon's atmosphere is very thin and gives no protection against rocks from space that smash into the surface. These impacts create large dips called craters. Some craters are huge and were made by rocks as big as mountains. Most of the Moon's surface is covered in dust. There are also parts called "seas" that are not water but dried lava that poured from volcanoes long ago.

Crescent Moon   Full Moon   Crescent Moon

ABOVE These are the Moon's phases as we see them throughout the month. The Moon's shape changes from a thin crescent to a circle and back again.

What are the Moon's phases?

The different shapes the Moon appears to take throughout the month are called the phases of the Moon. When we see the whole Moon, we call it a Full Moon. When we cannot see the Moon at all, we call it a New Moon. When we can see only a thin sliver of the Moon, we call it a crescent Moon. The Moon doesn't change shape—we just see different parts of it when it is in different stages of its orbit around Earth.

Who was the first on the Moon?

American astronaut Neil Armstrong was the first person on the Moon. As he left his landing craft on July 21, 1969, he said, "That's one small step for man but one giant leap for mankind." He and fellow astronaut Edwin "Buzz" Aldrin collected soil samples and took photos. The Moon's weak gravity made it easy to move around, but they had to wear space suits because there is no air there and the Sun's light is very strong.

21

DISCOVERING SPACE

Where is the world's biggest telescope?

The biggest telescopes in the world are at the Keck Observatories on the top of an extinct volcano in Hawaii. These two optical telescopes use mirrors instead of lenses to gather faint light from faraway galaxies. The main mirror in each telescope measures 33 feet across.

DID YOU KNOW?
Astronomers are planning to build bigger and bigger optical telescopes, with mirrors that are 100 to 300 feet wide.

Why do we need space telescopes?

When astronomers look through telescopes based on the Earth they have to look through our planet's cloudy, dusty atmosphere into space. Space telescopes sit above the atmosphere so that they can see into space more clearly. The Hubble Space telescope orbits at about 375 miles above the Earth. It has given astronomers incredibly clear views of our own solar system and faraway galaxies.

LEFT The Hubble Space telescope was launched in 1990.

How do space probes work?

Space probes are small, robot craft that are launched into space. They are programmed to fly past planets or land on them. Probes take photographs and use radar and other equipment to gather information. Then they send this information back to Earth using radio signals. In 2004, a NASA probe landed on Mars and sent back astonishing new pictures of the planet's surface.

What happens in a space station?

A space station is like a laboratory in space where astronauts study stars and other objects, and measure the way in which things, such as weightlessness, affect people. Astronauts travel to and from a space station on other spacecraft, and they live and work on board for weeks at a time. In addition to research laboratories and equipment, such as telescopes, a space station has living and eating quarters for the astronauts.

23

OUR EARTH

Mantle

Why does Earth have seasons?

Earth has seasons because it is tilted at an angle. This means that as it orbits around the Sun different parts are tilted toward the Sun. When the northern hemisphere, or top half of the Earth, points to the Sun, this area gets summer. At the same time, the southern hemisphere, or bottom half of the Earth, is pointing away from the Sun and this area experiences its winter.

LEFT Seen here is the same meadow in summer (top), fall (middle), and winter (bottom).

What causes night and day?

Night and day happen because Earth rotates, or makes one complete turn, every 24 hours. In addition to traveling in an orbit around the Sun, planet Earth spins around its axis, an imaginary line going through the North and South Poles. This means that at any one time, half of Earth is facing the Sun and is in daylight, while the other half faces away from the Sun, so is in night-time.

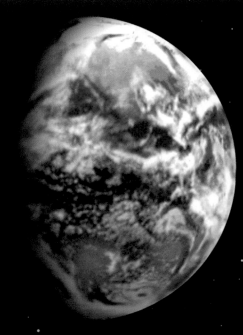

Outer core

What is inside the Earth?

Inside the center of the Earth there is red-hot, liquid rock. This rock is called magma. The land and oceans at the Earth's surface lie on an outer layer of cool, hard rock called the crust. The hot magma below rises and sinks slowly in a layer called the mantle. At the very center of the Earth is a superhot ball of iron called the core.

DID YOU KNOW?
The Earth's surface is cracked into large pieces, called plates, which fit together like an enormous jigsaw puzzle. There are nine large plates and several smaller ones.

Crust

Core

60 million years ago

How did the land divide into continents?

The land sits on top of the large pieces, or plates, that make up the Earth's surface. These plates are slowly moving. Before about 200 million years ago, all the land was joined to form one big continent, called a supercontinent. Over millions of years, as the plates moved, the land split and slowly divided into the seven continents we know today: Africa, Antarctica, Asia, Australia, Europe, North America, and South America.

155 million years ago

200 million years ago

25

VOLCANOES AND EARTHQUAKES

Why do volcanoes erupt?

Volcanoes erupt when some of the hot magma (liquid rock) from below the Earth's surface squeezes up through holes in the surface. Magma is so hot that it melts solid rock in its path and makes a tunnel through the crust just below the surface. Gradually, more and more magma builds up there, until suddenly the volcano erupts and the hot liquid rock spurts into the air.

What is a volcanic island?

When a volcano erupts on the ocean floor, the hot liquid rock cools and sets into hard rock. Each time the volcano erupts, it gets a little larger as more liquid rock piles up and hardens on its sides. Eventually, it becomes a tall underwater mountain with its tip sticking out above the water, forming an island.

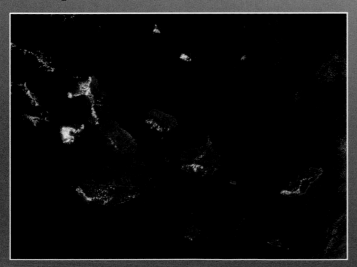

LEFT A string of islands can form when a plate in the Earth's crust glides slowly over a hole in the mantle where magma is released. The Galápagos Islands formed in this way.

26

RIGHT Most earthquakes last for less than a minute, but their force can be felt over a huge area.

Why do earthquakes happen?

Earthquakes happen because the plates that make up the Earth's crust are moving like giant rafts on the bubbling magma below. These plates usually slide against each other gently, but sometimes two plates get stuck and push hard against each other. When they suddenly jolt apart again, this sudden movement creates the violent shaking at the Earth's surface known as earthquakes.

How do earthquakes cause damage?

BELOW Tsunamis are giant waves caused by earthquakes underwater. They can cause great damage when they hit the shore, leaving behind wrecked homes.

When small earthquakes shake the land they may simply knock books off shelves, but large earthquakes can make buildings and roads crumble. They can create huge cracks in the land into which whole lakes disappear. Some earthquakes set off landslides, where huge amounts of soil slide down a hill and bury buildings at the bottom.

MOUNTAINS AND VALLEYS

How do mountains form?

Some mountains form from volcanoes. Dome mountains occur where magma near the Earth's surface forms a rounded bulge of rock but does not erupt to become a volcano. Fold mountains form when two colliding plates cause the Earth's crust to buckle and fold, making mountain ranges. Block mountains form when fractures in the Earth's crust push a block of rock upward.

Do mountains continue to grow?

Yes, some mountains continue to get taller after they first form! For example, the Himalayas are growing by just over 2 inches every year. The Himalayas were formed 50 million years ago when two of the Earth's plates collided. As the plates continue to push into each other the mountains are gradually getting higher—and they are getting even harder to climb!

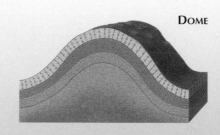
DOME

FOLD

BLOCK

DID YOU KNOW?
The Mid-Atlantic Ocean Ridge is an underwater mountain range. It is as long as the Rocky, Andes, and Himalaya mountain ranges combined.

What is a glacier?

A glacier is a huge river of ice. A buildup of snow and ice in very cold, high mountain areas causes the river of ice to flow downhill. Most glaciers flow so slowly you cannot tell they are moving. As glaciers move, they carry rocks along with them that help gouge out valleys, or deep grooves, into the land through which they pass.

Mountain glaciers have created many of the valleys on the Earth's surface.

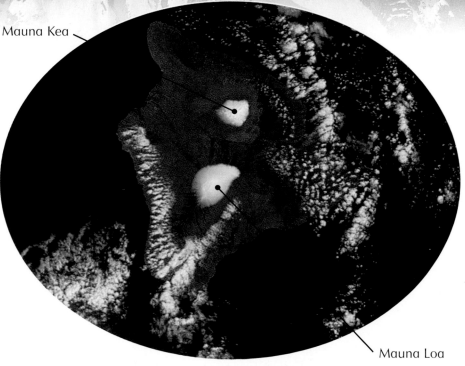

Mauna Kea

Mauna Loa

Where is the tallest mountain?

The tallest mountain is Mauna Kea on Hawaii. It measures 33,375 feet from base to peak, but most of it is underwater. Only 13,795 feet of it are above sea level. On land, Mount Everest is the highest mountain, reaching 29,035 feet above sea level. Also on Hawaii is Mauna Loa, the world's biggest volcano.

SHAPING THE EARTH

What is weathering?

Weathering is the wearing away of rock at the Earth's surface. Weathering can be caused by wind, frost, rain, and heat from the Sun. Weathering can even change the shape of mountains. When rain seeps into cracks in rocks it may turn to ice. Ice takes up more space than water and the ice makes the cracks bigger. Eventually, weathering breaks off whole pieces of rock and they fall away.

BELOW The Grand Canyon is 275 miles long. In places, it is 15 miles wide and over 1 mile deep.

How was the Grand Canyon formed?

The Grand Canyon in Arizona is the largest valley on Earth and was created by water. The force and weight of the water shapes the land through which a river flows. The water wears away pieces of rock and these pieces help the river scratch away deeper into the land. This is how the Colorado River gradually carved out the Grand Canyon over many centuries.

When do sand dunes form?

Sand dunes form when the wind blows small, light grains of sand into hills and mounds along coastlines and in deserts. Sand is made when rocks are weathered by wind and water. As stones are tossed together in the water, or blown into each other by the wind, they gradually break up. They get smaller and smaller, until eventually they become grains of sand.

Why is the coastline shrinking?

Coastlines all around the world are shrinking because of the power of the sea. As waves crash against shorelines, they wear away rocks at the bottom of cliffs. When these rocks break away, the upper part of the cliff falls into the sea, too. The waves crash these pieces of rock together and break them into small pieces that the water washes away.

DID YOU KNOW?
In some places, many years of weathering has worn away entire mountains.

31

THE EARTH'S ATMOSPHERE

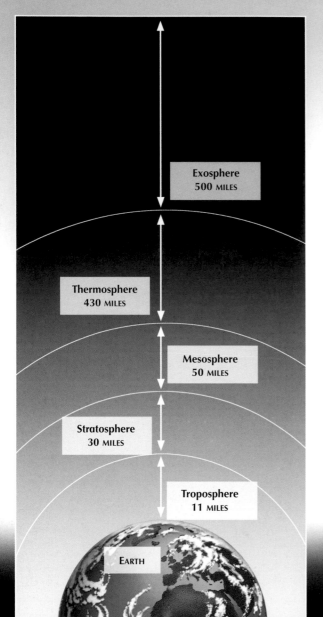

Exosphere
500 MILES

Thermosphere
430 MILES

Mesosphere
50 MILES

Stratosphere
30 MILES

Troposphere
11 MILES

EARTH

Where is the atmosphere?

The atmosphere is the layer of air that surrounds the Earth. It is like a blanket of gases wrapped around the planet. One of the most important gases in the atmosphere is oxygen, which all living things need to live. The atmosphere protects the Earth by filtering out harmful rays from the Sun. The atmosphere is divided into smaller layers. The nearest one to the Earth is the troposphere.

What is air pressure?

Air pressure is the weight of the air in the atmosphere that presses down on the Earth. The amount of air pressure varies at different places on the Earth. If you are up a mountain, there is less air above you, so the air pressure is less. We do not usually feel the weight of the air pressing down on us because air within our bodies pushes out, balancing the pressure with the air outside.

ABOVE Mountaineers sometimes carry oxygen bottles because the air is thinner and it can be harder to breathe high up a mountain.

How does the greenhouse effect work?

Some gases in the atmosphere are known as greenhouse gases because they keep our planet warm, similar to the way greenhouse glass keeps plants inside warm. When heat from the Sun hits the Earth, much of it bounces back into the sky. Greenhouse gases stop the Sun's warmth from escaping into space and reflect the heat back to the Earth.

Sun

Atmosphere

Some of the Sun's rays are reflected back into space or absorbed by the atmosphere.

Some of the Sun's rays hit the Earth.

Some heat escapes into space.

Some heat bounces back to Earth.

DID YOU KNOW?
Without the greenhouse gases in the atmosphere, heat would escape back into space and Earth's average temperature would be about 95 degrees Fahrenheit colder.

Why is global warming a problem?

Global warming is an increase in world temperatures caused by the greenhouse effect. It is a problem because the extra heat in the atmosphere leads to more severe weather, such as storms and floods. The heat also causes polar ice to melt, leading to rising sea levels. Humans are contributing to the problem by burning fuels that pump more greenhouse gases into the atmosphere.

WEATHER AND CLIMATE

What is climate?

A region's climate is the type of weather it gets throughout the year. Scientists split the world into five major climate zones. Tropical areas have hot, wet climates. Areas with dry climates get little rain. Temperate areas have cool winters and warm summers. Continental climates have cold winters and mild summers. Polar climates have freezing temperatures all year round.

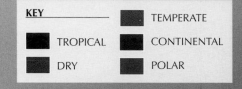

KEY
- TROPICAL
- DRY
- TEMPERATE
- CONTINENTAL
- POLAR

EQUATOR

ABOVE This map shows where the world's five main climate zones are found.

DID YOU KNOW?
In freezing conditions, water falling from the sky becomes snow or hail. Hailstones are balls of ice and some can be the size of a large grapefruit!

Why do winds blow?

Wind is moving air, and winds blow when air temperatures change. When the Sun shines, it heats a patch of air. Warm air is lighter than cold air, so the warm air rises. Cooler air moves into the spaces the warm air left behind. These air movements are what we know as wind. When air moves quickly it can be a howling gale. Small air movements can create a gentle breeze.

When does it rain?

Raindrops are part of the water cycle—the continuous movement of water between Earth and sky. When the Sun heats water on the surface of oceans and lakes some of it turns into water vapor, a gas in the air. When water vapor rises high in the air, where it is cold, it cools and turns into water droplets. These gather in clouds, then fall back to Earth as rain. The cycle then begins again.

Water vapor collects to form clouds.

Water falls as rain.

Water turns into water vapor.

Water flows into seas.

Water flows downhill in streams and rivers.

How do people forecast weather?

Meteorologists are scientists who study the weather. They have many ways of predicting the weather. They use balloons that float in the air to record temperature and humidity (the amount of water in the air). They use photographs of the Earth taken from space so they can see the direction in which storms are blowing. Weather stations around the world share data through computers in order to keep people informed about the weather.

DINOSAURS AND PREHISTORIC LIFE

Three hundred million years before humans first stood upright, reptiles known as dinosaurs ruled supreme. Some evolved to become the largest land animals ever to walk the Earth. Others were savage predators. The dinosaurs' reign ended about 65 million years ago, probably when a meteorite smashed into the Earth and caused them to become extinct. In the periods that followed, mammals were the dominant species, evolving to include some amazing creatues, including, finally, us.

RECORD IN THE ROCKS

What is a fossil?

A fossil is the remains of a plant or animal that lived millions of years ago. Fossils are a record of what lived on the Earth in prehistoric times, the period before humans existed or began to write about the world. Without fossils, we would not know about ancient living things, such as dinosaurs.

ABOVE Some fossils are insects that were trapped in tree sap. The sap hardened to form amber such as this.

DID YOU KNOW?
People have found fossils of sea creatures at the tops of mountains. This is because, over millions of years, the seabed was lifted up and formed mountains. Weather wore the rock away, exposing the fossils.

How do fossils form?

Fossils form in different ways. Some fossils form when an animal, such as a shellfish, dies. It sinks to the bottom of the sea and is slowly covered in muddy sediment. Over millions of years, the sediment hardens into rock. Meanwhile, the animal's body rots away and is replaced by mineral substances. As these harden they form rock shaped like the animal. This is called a fossil cast.

Millions of years ago, a sea creature called an ammonite dies.

It sinks to the bottom of the sea and is covered in sediment.

The ammonite rots away and minerals replace it.

The minerals harden into rock and form a fossil.

When is the oldest fossil from?

The oldest fossils that have been found are from around 3.5 billion years ago. These fossils are also the smallest ever found. They are the remains of bacteria, tiny living things that formed a kind of slime in ancient pools and seas. The oldest fossils with hard parts, such as shells, are about 545 million years old.

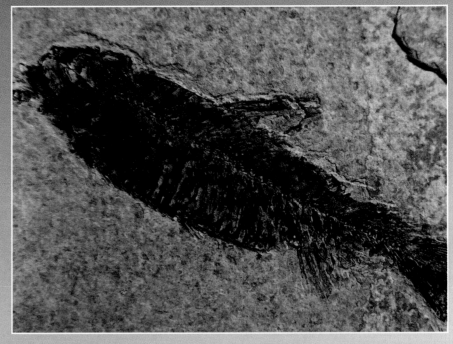

ABOVE Many fossils are of fish and other sea creatures because most fossils formed in the sea.

BELOW These fossil footsteps were left by a prehistoric creature millions of years ago.

What do fossils tell us?

Fossils tell us a lot about the plants and animals that lived long ago. For example, by piecing together fossil dinosaur bones, scientists have learned how dinosaurs moved and hunted. Using fossils, they can tell when some animals died out and when new kinds of animals first appeared. Fossils help scientists understand how life on Earth grew from a few tiny living things to the great variety we know today.

THE BEGINNING OF LIFE

When did life on Earth begin?

Life on Earth began about 3.5 billion years ago.
When the Earth first formed, it was too hot for life to exist.
The first living things were bacteria, which developed in
deep-sea springs or muddy pools near volcanoes (right),
after the Earth had cooled. The bacteria took their energy
from chemicals in water and slowly developed into more
complex life forms, a process known as evolution.

ABOVE Stromatolites are layers
of blue-green algae and rock.
These algae were among the
earliest living things to make
food by photosynthesis.

How did living things develop?

Many new living things began to develop by 3 billion years
ago, after some early life forms found a way of getting
energy from sunlight and using it to make food. This process
is called photosynthesis. During photosynthesis, living
things release the gas oxygen. Many more living things then
developed to breathe the new oxygen in the atmosphere.

Ernietta

Charnia

Spriggina

What were the first animals like?

The first animals probably looked a little like tiny tadpoles. They lived in the shallow seas that covered the Earth about 1.2 billion years ago and thrived on the new supplies of oxygen in the atmosphere. Slowly, these tiny animals grew together in clusters and developed into the first sponges.

DID YOU KNOW?
Some of the kinds of animals that first lived long ago still exist today, such as the starfish. However, most are extinct, which means they all died out.

Where did early animals live?

Early animals, such as sponges, jellyfish, and sea pens, all lived on the sea floor. They fed on parts of dead plants and animals in the mud or water. At this stage, there was no need for them to move because there were no predators (hunters).

Pteridinium

Jelly blobs

Cyclomedusa

Parvancorina

Tribrachidium

Dickinsonia

ABOVE Early animals lived on the sea floor and had no need to move.

UNDERWATER LIFE

When did ammonites live?

Ammonites lived about 400 million years ago. They were sea animals with a hard spiral shell, and they probably floated slowly through the sea. Some ammonites were as big as semi-truck wheels. At this time, the oceans were full of sea animals with shells of many different shapes and sizes. Some creatures even had two shells.

RIGHT Some of the largest ammonites weighed up to 220 pounds.

DID YOU KNOW?
Nautiloids were the ancestors of modern squid and octopuses. They used jets of water to push themselves quickly through the sea after prey.

What were trilobites?

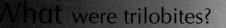

Trilobites were ancient animals that looked like giant wood lice. Their bodies were divided into three segments, or parts, and they had armored skin. They scurried across ocean floors, looking for food. About 400 million years ago, trilobites of all shapes and sizes roamed the seas. At the same time, other segmented animals, such as crabs and lobsters, developed. Trilobites died out about 250 million years ago.

Which animals are called sea lilies?

The animals called sea lilies look something like armor-plated starfish on tall stalks. They developed 500 million years ago and are still with us today. They got their name because they wave their tentacles in the water to trap food. This makes them look similar to flowers. Sea lilies attach themselves to the seabed. The largest are 65 feet long.

How do coral reefs form?

Coral reefs are formed by tiny animals known as polyps, which are a little like sea anemones. The coral polyps live together in large groups called colonies. Together, they form hard external skeletons to support their bodies. The skeletons slowly build up into large mounds known as coral reefs. The reefs become underwater habitats for many sea creatures.

RIGHT Trilobites were one of many sea creatures that lived on the ancient coral reefs.

Trilobite

PREHISTORIC FISH

Did fish always have jaws?

No, the first fish had no jaws. These jawless fish developed over 500 million years ago. Without jaws to open and close their mouths, they fed by sucking up food particles from the mud. They had no fins either, so they probably swam like stiff tadpoles, wiggling their bodies and flat tails left and right to move through the water. The only jawless fish that exist today are hagfish and lampreys.

ABOVE The first fish had no jaws, so they could only feed by sucking up food.

When did fish develop jaws?

About 425 million years ago, new kinds of fish developed that had jaws. With jaws, these fish could bite and tear off pieces of food. The first fish with jaws that have been found as fossils were the acanthodians. These were small but fierce fish with stiff spiny fins. They used their tail fins to push themselves through the water. They also had overlapping scales on their bodies like modern fish.

Which fish had armor plating?

Several of the smaller kinds of early fish had bodies covered in armor plating. These hard shell-like plates helped to protect the fish from predators, such as large jellyfish and giant sea scorpions. The flexible tails stuck out at the back and swung from side to side to move the fish along.

BELOW Armor plating covered the bodies of some smaller fish.

BELOW The coelacanth was thought to be extinct but some people in Africa had long known of it.

What fish is known as the living fossil?

The coelacanth is known as a living fossil. It is a prehistoric fish still found in the sea today. It was one of the most common early jawed fish. For a long time many people thought that the coelacanth had become extinct 70 million years ago. Then, in 1938, a fisherman caught a living coelacanth in the Indian Ocean.

GIANT FORESTS AND INSECTS

ABOVE A fossilized fern.

When did plants first grow on land?

Plants first began to grow on land around 475 million years ago. These plants lived in swamps and on the muddy shores of rivers. They probably had a waxy coating to stop the salty water and the sun from drying them out. Plants gradually developed roots to reach water underground. They soon spread beyond the shores and began to turn the land green.

Why did early plants grow so big?

Early plants were able to grow so big because of the climate long ago. In many places, the air was damp and steamy, kind of like it is in tropical jungles today. As plants crowded together, they grew taller and taller as they competed for the light. Plants in the great early forests included huge horsetails, club mosses, and ferns up to 165 feet tall. That is as high as 9 giraffes stacked on top of each other!

DID YOU KNOW?
Over millions of years, the giant trees and plants from the swamps of this time rotted and hardened to form the coal we burn today.

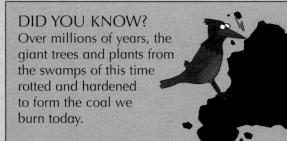

Tree fern

RIGHT This giant swampy forest is from about 300 million years ago. Some plants and insects were much bigger than their relatives alive today.

What were the first insects like?

The first insects were probably the bristletails, which were the size of a large shrimp. They had no wings and scurried around the ancient swamps on little legs. They used their bristles to sense movements in the air, which warned them a predator, or hunter was around. They had claws on their mouthparts which they used to eat plants and waste.

How big were the first dragonflies?

Some of the first dragonflies had a wingspan of up to a yard. They flew over pools, using their large eyes to look for other insects to eat. Winged insects first appeared around 400 million years ago. They could explore more places to live and find different kinds of food. Soon, many more insect species developed, including cockroaches and grasshoppers.

ABOVE A fossilized dragonfly.

Giant horsetail

Dragonfly

Club moss

THE FIRST FOUR-LEGGED

When did four legs develop?

Four-legged animals first appeared about 370 million years ago. These ancestors of amphibians, reptiles, and mammals evolved from fish. Scientists know that these fish had fins that they used for walking on muddy riverbeds. They may have scrambled out of shallow water to catch insects or snails. Slowly, their stubby fins evolved into strong legs.

RIGHT This mud-skipper is a modern fish that can swim in water and move around on land. All four-legged animals evolved from fish similar to this.

How big were early four-legged animals?

Early four-legged animals, known as tetrapods, ranged in size from about 10 inches to 10 feet in length. One, called *Cacops*, was about 16 inches long and had a long tail and a thick armor of bony plates on its back to defend itself against attack. *Diadectes* was a heavy, 10-feet-long beast that probably looked very fierce, but it used its teeth for munching plants.

BELOW *Pantylus*, one of the smallest early amphibians, was about 10 inches long.

Which tetrapod had a triangular head?

The early tetrapod with a triangular head was called *Diplocaulus*. Some scientists think that this odd-looking animal had a boomerang-shaped head to make it difficult for predators, or hunters, to swallow. Others think the shape may have developed to help *Diplocaulus* rise and sink rapidly in the water when it was chasing insects and fish to eat.

BELOW A tadpole is born with a tail, but it soon grows legs, ready for when it will live on land.

DID YOU KNOW?
Other groups of amphibians, such as newts and salamanders, evolved around 200 million years ago and would have been running under the feet of dinosaurs that lived around the same time.

Where do amphibians breed?

Although they live on land as adults, amphibians return to the water to breed. This is as true of the early tetrapods as it is of today's amphibians, such as frogs and toads. The first frogs developed about 200 million years ago. They laid soft-skinned eggs underwater. The tadpoles that hatched from these eggs had gills for breathing and tails for swimming. Like tadpoles today, they later developed lungs and legs for life on land.

49

RISE OF THE REPTILES

What was the first reptile?

The first reptile was probably *Hylonomus*, which lived 315 million years ago. *Hylonomus* was 8 inches long and looked a little like a modern lizard. Reptiles like these evolved from a group of amphibian-like tetrapods that laid their eggs on land. Inside the eggs, the young fed on yolks, which made them strong and more likely to survive. Reptiles soon became the dominant animals on land.

RIGHT *Hylonomus* used its small sharp teeth to eat millipedes and early insects.

Which reptiles had armored bodies?

BELOW This early turtle had a heavily armored shell.

The group of reptiles known as pareiasaurs had plates of bony armor over their bodies. They lived about 260 million years ago. One type of pareiasaur was *Scutosaurus*, which means "shield lizard." Although it grew to about 10 feet long and was large and powerful, it was a plant eater. Some of the first tortoises and turtles, which evolved about 50 million years later, were as big as *Scutosaurus*.

Why did *Dimetrodon* have a sail on its back?

Scientists do not know for sure why *Dimetrodon* had a spiny sail on its back. Perhaps this reptilelike creature used the sail to soak up warmth from the sun when it was cold or to give off heat to cool down on hot days. Other theories are that it could have been used to attract mates or to scare off other animals.

LEFT *Dimetrodon*'s spiny sail probably helped it to warm up and cool down.

DID YOU KNOW?
Some of the people who think that the Loch Ness Monster really exists believe it may be descended from a plesiosaur.

BELOW Ichthyosaurs were sleek, fast-swimming reptiles.

Did early reptiles ever live in water?

Some early reptiles lived permanently in water. The plesiosaurs had large paddlelike legs for moving through the water and long necks for reaching out to catch fish. Ichthyosaurs looked more like large, toothy dolphins. They were swimming in the oceans at the same time as dinosaurs were living on the land.

DAWN OF THE DINOSAURS

When did dinosaurs develop?

The first dinosaurs developed from other reptiles about 230 million years ago. At this time, the world looked very different. There were no birds or mammals, and, although there were ferns and trees, there were no grasses or flowering plants. Vast areas were desert. Dinosaurs dominated the world for 150 million years.

DID YOU KNOW?
Scientists may never be sure what color dinosaurs were or even whether some had hair.

Brachiosaurus

Why did dinosaurs get so big?

Scientists are not certain why some dinosaurs got so big. Dinosaurs may have developed into larger, stronger, and faster animals in order to compete with each other for food. Sauropods were by far the biggest dinosaurs, with long necks to reach leaves at the tops of tall trees. The carnivores may simply have evolved into larger beasts to be able to catch them.

ABOVE *Brachiosaurus* was one of the largest sauropods—gigantic, slow-moving plant eaters. Sauropods included some of the biggest land animals of all time.

Did any dinosaurs live in water?

No, dinosaurs only lived on land. Some reptiles did live in the sea, including *Plesiosaursus*, which was not related to dinosaurs. This large carnivorous animal had a long neck and sharp teeth to catch fish. Other reptiles, such as the pterosaurs, could fly. They had wings made of skin, similar to those of bats.

LEFT *Plesiosaurus* lived in the sea and could grow up to 40 feet long.

What was the smallest dinosaur?

The smallest dinosaurs were not much bigger than a chicken. *Saltopus*, which lived about 220 million years ago, was about 2 feet long and scurried along the ground eating insects. *Compsognathus*, which means "pretty jaw," lived about 150 million years ago and was only about 3 feet long.

Compsognathus

DINOSAUR RULE

Which dinosaur waddled?

The giant *Megalosaurus* dinosaur probably waddled like a duck. Its tail would have swung to and fro as it walked along. *Megalosaurus* lived in the Jurassic period, when dinosaurs dominated the Earth. It had vicious claws and saw-edged teeth for cutting into the flesh of its prey.

LEFT *Megalosaurus* had saw-edged teeth for cutting into flesh.

Why did *Stegosaurus* have armored plates?

The rows of armored plates along *Stegosaurus*'s back probably helped make the dinosaur look bigger to keep predators away. Some scientists think that the plates may have been used to display to other stegosaurs. Another group of dinosaurs, the ankylosaurs, also had armored plates. They even had armored eyelids.

RIGHT *Stegosaurus* used its spiked tail for defense and its beaked mouth to bite off plants to eat.

DID YOU KNOW?
Argentinosaurus and many other dinosaurs were huge, but the blue whale is bigger than any of them.

How fast could dinosaurs run?

Some dinosaurs, such as *Gallimimus*, may have run up to 40 miles an hour. *Gallimimus* was an ostrichlike dinosaur that probably lived in groups. It had a small head with a toothless, beaked mouth and probably ate insects, small animals, and eggs. It had long legs and a long tail that helped it to keep its balance when making fast, sharp turns.

ABOVE *Gallimimus* was up to 115 feet long and about 12 feet tall.

Did dinosaurs hunt in packs?

Yes, some dinosaurs might have hunted in packs, working together in order to catch and bring down larger dinosaurs. *Giganotosaurus* was one of the biggest meat-eating dinosaurs ever. It could hunt alone, but to catch a full-grown *Argentinosaurus*, perhaps the largest dinosaur that ever lived, packs of six or more *Giganotosaurus* worked together.

BELOW *Argentinosaurus* grew to over 115 feet long. Even so, it was prey to *Giganotosaurus*.

THE LAST DINOSAURS

Which dinosaur had the biggest claws?

Therizinosaurus had the biggest claws. This dinosaur had three curved claws on each of its arms, measuring up to 3 feet long. It was a herbivore, or plant eater, and it may have used its claws to pull down branches from high trees to eat the bark and leaves.

BELOW *Therizinosaurus* used its enormous claws to reach branches on tall trees.

DID YOU KNOW?
Some of the most common later dinosaurs were the hadrosaurs. They had a toothless beak that looked like that of a duck and are called duck-billed dinosaurs.

RIGHT *Tyrannosaurus rex*'s teeth could grow to 12 inches long.

How many teeth did *Tyrannosaurus rex* have?

Tyrannosaurus rex had over 60 thick, cone-shaped teeth in its yard-long mouth. Some of the teeth were sharp as knives and used to slice off flesh. Others were shaped for crunching bones, so that the animals could eat the bone marrow inside the bones. Although *Tyrannosaurus rex* is often seen as a fierce and successful hunter, it may also have been a scavenger, eating animals it found that were already dead.

When did *Triceratops* use its horns?

Triceratops probably used its horns to protect itself. When attacked, it probably stood its ground and used them to injure a predator. At about 30 feet long, *Triceratops* was a large plant eater. It may even have been able to take on the mighty *Tyrannosaurus rex*. Scientists think that the bony frill around their necks enabled the different *Triceratops* in a herd to tell each other apart.

BELOW *Triceratops* used its horns for defense.

Why did dinosaurs die out?

There are several theories about why dinosaurs died out about 65 million years ago. The main one is that a giant asteroid crashed into the Earth around this time. The impact would have created dust, fires, tsunamis (giant waves), and volcanic eruptions that caused a huge change in the planet's climate. It seems likely that the world became freezing cold, and the dinosaurs simply could not survive in the icy conditions.

BELOW Scientists think an asteroid may have crashed into the Earth, killing some dinosaurs immediately. Others died later as the climate changed.

EARLY BIRDS

How did birds develop?

Scientists believe that birds developed from dinosaurs. They have discovered the fossil remains of feathered dinosaurs that many people believe proves birds are descended from dinosaurs. The fossils were of dromaeosaur dinosaurs. They could not fly but had fluffy down on their bodies and short arms covered with feathers.

DID YOU KNOW?
Hesperornis had webbed feet and small wings for swimming and diving. Its long jaws had many sharp teeth for catching fish and ammonites.

LEFT Fossils show that dromaeosaurs had wrist joints that worked much like those in the wing of a modern bird.

What is the oldest known bird?

Archaeopteryx is the oldest known bird in the world. It flew in ancient skies about 150 million years ago. It was a meat-eating bird about the size of a crow, and it probably flew fairly short distances at a time. It had feathers like a bird, but it also had teeth and clawed hands like a dinosaur.

RIGHT A fossil of an *Archaeopteryx*.

Which was the largest bird?

The largest of the prehistoric birds was *Aepyornis*, also called the elephant bird. It was 10 feet tall and weighed about 1,000 pounds. It also laid the biggest eggs of all time—some were almost 3 feet long. Another flightless bird was *Dinornis*, which grew to 12 feet high. It was the tallest bird that ever lived. Both birds had strong, thick legs, a long neck, and a bulky body.

BELOW *Aepyornis* looked a little like a modern ostrich.

What was the monster bird?

The monster bird was *Teratornis*, a prehistoric creature that looked something like a giant condor. It had a wingspan of roughly 16 to 23 feet. It flew around searching for the dead bodies of other animals to eat. Its remains have been found in tar pits in California, where the bird was presumably trapped when it came down to feed.

RIGHT Like modern vultures, *Teratornis* fed on dead or dying animals.

THE RISE OF MAMMALS

When did mammals develop?

The first mammals developed almost 200 million years ago. During the time of the dinosaurs, mammals were small, furry creatures. They looked something like the rats and shrews of today, and they ate insects. They scurried around at night and probably lived in holes underground to hide from dinosaurs. After the dinosaurs died out, many new kinds of mammal slowly developed.

BELOW The first mammal was probably *Megazostrodon*, a small ratlike animal.

Did early mammals lay eggs?

Some early mammals laid eggs, unlike most modern mammals, which give birth to live young. Mammals evolved from mammal-like reptiles that grew fur as mammals do, but laid eggs like a reptile. Some prehistoric mammals, such as the giant prehistoric kangaroos, were marsupials. Marsupials give birth to very tiny young, which complete their development in a pouch on their mothers' bodies.

RIGHT The modern platypus lays eggs, as early mammals did.

What was the largest meat-eating mammal?

The fierce carnivore *Andrewsarchus* was the largest meat-eating land mammal ever. It was almost 7 feet tall and 16 feet long. *Andrewsarchus* was a doglike animal with long, powerful jaws. Its teeth were very strong for biting through bone and turtle shell, and it probably searched for food at the edge of rivers.

BELOW *Andrewsarchus* was a doglike prehistoric mammal.

DID YOU KNOW?
Some scientists believe that the sudden increase in the amount of oxygen on Earth about 50 million years ago explains why bigger mammals, such as huge saber-toothed cats, evolved.

BELOW *Glyptodon* had an armored body and grew to 10 feet long.

Do all mammals have teeth?

No, most mammals have teeth, but there is a strange group that have few or no teeth. These are the edentates and include armadillos, sloths, and anteaters. One of these was the giant *Glyptodon*, the last of which died 10,000 years ago. *Glyptodon* had no teeth at the front of its mouth, but it had strange globe-shaped teeth at the back for grinding plant foods. It could grow to the size of a car.

GIANT GRAZERS

Who were the giant grazers?

The giant grazers were prehistoric herbivores—plant eaters—that reached gigantic sizes. From about 130 million years ago, a whole new range of flowering plants and trees developed on Earth. Vast areas of grasses spread, and these provided food for many different herbivores, such as giant rhinos and *Megaloceros*, whose name means "giant antler."

RIGHT *Megaloceros* had such huge antlers that some scientists think they caused its extinction. The antlers may have grown so big that the animals could not lift their heads.

LEFT *Phoberomys pattersoni* were so big and slow that they were easy for predators to catch, so they died out.

Were there giant guinea pigs?

Yes, about eight million years ago, giant guinea pigs called *Phoberomys pattersoni* roamed riverbanks grazing on aquatic grass. Unfortunately, their huge size may be the reason they died out. They were almost as large as cows and couldn't move quickly enough to escape from fierce or fast-moving hunters such as giant crocodiles, lion-sized cats, and monstrous flesh-eating birds.

How were prehistoric rhinos different?

BELOW The woolly rhino had two huge horns on its head to protect itself.

Some prehistoric rhinoceroses were different from those around today because they were woolly. The long-haired woolly rhino first appeared 350,000 years ago and may have survived until as recently as 10,000 years ago. This plant eater was about 12 feet long. Prehistoric paintings found on cave walls tell us that woolly rhinos were hunted by early humans.

DID YOU KNOW?
The number of flowering plants and insects increased at about the same time because flowers need insects to reproduce (through a process called pollination) and insects need flowers for food.

Why were mammoths woolly?

Woolly mammoths had a coat of woolly hair to keep them warm. About 30,000 years ago, there was an ice age, and to survive the freezing conditions, many animals, including mammoths and saber-toothed tigers, grew extra hair. The remains of woolly mammoths have been found frozen in icy regions of Siberia.

RIGHT Woolly mammoths put on weight in summer, and lived off the stored fat in winter.

FROM APES TO HUMANS

What are primates?

Primates are a group of mammals that includes apes, monkeys, and humans. The first primates lived on Earth about 50 million years ago, but they looked something like squirrels. Over millions of years, different kinds of primates evolved. Between 20 and 10 million years ago, giant apes were common in Africa.

LEFT A giant Asian ape called *Gigantopithecus*.

LEFT Male Neanderthals were heavily built and stood about 5 feet, 5 inches tall.

Who were the Neanderthals?

The Neanderthals were an ancient human species that lived in Europe and Asia from about 300,000 to 30,000 years ago, when they became extinct. Long ago, there were other human species, but all of these died out. One was *Homo erectus*, perhaps our earliest human ancestor. *Homo erectus* first appeared almost two million years ago and died out 100,000 years ago.

How did the first people live?

The first people depended on wild plants and animals for food. They used sharp sticks to spear animals or knock them from trees. Their use of tools and their ability to work together were two of the things that made early humans so successful. These early hunters may even have driven some kinds of prehistoric animals to extinction.

BELOW People began to grow their own food and keep animals, such as goats, about 10,000 years ago.

DID YOU KNOW?
Bodies of humans that died as long as 2,300 years ago have been found perfectly preserved in peat bogs. These remains can tell us a great deal about how people lived long ago.

Why did people start farming?

Prehistoric people probably started farming because it was easier than traveling a long way to chase wild animals or gather berries and nuts. As people settled in one place, the first villages and towns developed. About 5,000 years ago, people began to read and write. This was the end of the prehistoric period, because people started to write down their history.

PLANTS AND ANIMALS

There are millions of different kinds of plants and animals living in every place on Earth. They range in size from tiny microscopic plants and animals that are too small to see with the naked eye, to massive whales and giant trees. All of these living things have found ways of surviving in their habitats, whether they live in the blackness of the deep ocean, the heat of the desert, or the cold of the mountaintops.

TYPES OF LIVING THINGS

What is a living thing?

Something is said to be a living thing because it can do certain things. It can reproduce, which means it can have young. It can grow and change during its life and use energy from food to live and stay healthy. A living thing can also move in a variety of ways and sense the world around it.

ABOVE These gazelles are living things because they grow, eat, move, and reproduce.

BELOW Sunflowers make seeds in the center of their large flowers. Ferns produce spores on special leaves.

Fern

Do all plants have flowers?

No, but most do! Flowering plants, such as sunflowers and oak trees, reproduce from seeds made in their flowers. Non-flowering plants use different ways to reproduce. For example, pine trees and other conifers make their seeds in cones. Ferns, mosses, and seaweeds make tiny grains called spores, usually on their leaves. Spores can only grow into new plants in wet or damp places.

Sunflower

How many different animals are there?

We know of more than a million different kinds of animal on Earth. Scientists make it easier to identify and understand animals by classifying them, or putting them into groups, based on similarities. Animals are classified into two main groups: vertebrates, which have a backbone, and invertebrates, which do not. Vertebrates include humans, snakes, and birds. Invertebrates include insects, worms, and snails.

DID YOU KNOW?
The seeds of the coco de mer palm tree are the biggest in the world. They can weigh up to 93 pounds—the same as a large dog.

ABOVE A howler monkey is a vertebrate.

A frog is an amphibian.

Which kinds of vertebrates are which?

Vertebrates are classified into five groups: fish, reptiles, amphibians, birds, and mammals. Fish and reptiles both have scaly skin, but fish live in water and reptiles live on land. Amphibians have smooth skin and, although they live on land as adults, their young live in water. Birds have feathers and their young hatch from hard eggs. Mammals usually have hair and feed their young on milk.

A chimp is a mammal.

An eagle is a bird.

A snake is a reptile.

A cichlid is a fish.

FEEDING AND LIVING

Why do flowers need bees?

Flowering plants need bees and other insects to help them reproduce. Bees visit flowers to feed on their sweet nectar. Pollen collects on a bee's legs when it lands on a flower. When the bee visits another flower, some of this pollen rubs onto the flower. That flower uses the pollen to make seeds that will grow into new plants. Many of the plants and animals that live in the same place need each other to survive.

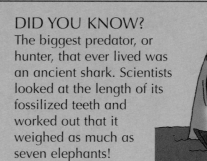

DID YOU KNOW?
The biggest predator, or hunter, that ever lived was an ancient shark. Scientists looked at the length of its fossilized teeth and worked out that it weighed as much as seven elephants!

How do plants make their food?

Plants make their own food inside their leaves through a process called photosynthesis. The ingredients plants use are water, which is sucked up through the roots, and carbon dioxide, a gas in the air. The leaves absorb sunlight and use this energy to make food from the ingredients. Plants store this sugary food inside them until they need to use it.

Do all animals eat meat?

No, some animals eat only meat, some eat only plants, and some eat both plants and meat. Animals that eat only meat, such as sharks and cats, are called carnivores. Most carnivores have sharp teeth or claws to catch animals. Animals that eat only plants, such as cows and caterpillars, are called herbivores. Animals that eat both meat and plants, such as humans, are called omnivores.

BELOW Sharks are some of the fiercest hunters in the ocean. They have excellent senses, which help them find animals to eat.

What is a food chain?

A food chain is a way of showing what eats what in a particular place. The start of any food chain is a plant, which makes its food by photosynthesis. Next is an animal that eats the plant. Then comes another animal, called a predator, that eats the plant eater. The animal at the end of a food chain is not eaten by any other animal.

BELOW In this food chain, lions eat zebras, which eat grass. The arrows in the food chain point to the animal that does the eating.

HABITATS OF THE WORLD

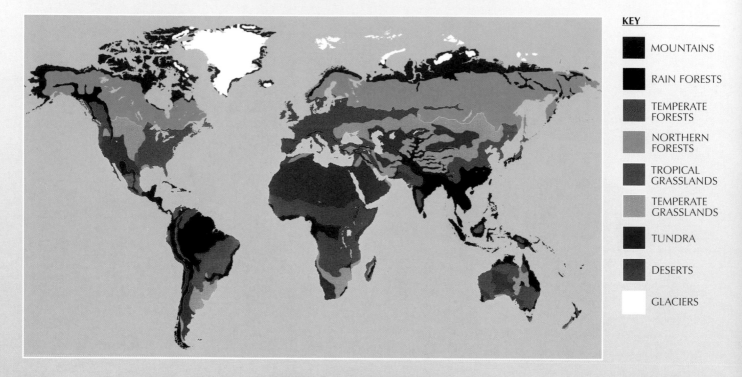

KEY

- MOUNTAINS
- RAIN FORESTS
- TEMPERATE FORESTS
- NORTHERN FORESTS
- TROPICAL GRASSLANDS
- TEMPERATE GRASSLANDS
- TUNDRA
- DESERTS
- GLACIERS

BELOW Coral reefs are a type of habitat found in the oceans.

What is a habitat?

A habitat is a place where plants and animals live. There are many different kinds of habitat around the world. Habitats are different because of the weather and the temperature. For example, mountains are windy and cold and deserts are dry and hot. The map shows the main land habitats, which include mountains, rain forests, temperate forests, northern forests, grasslands, tundra, and deserts. Other habitats, not shown on the map, include the oceans, lakes, rivers, and coasts.

Which is the world's biggest habitat?

The oceans are the world's biggest habitat. They cover three-quarters of the Earth's surface and are full of life. Some animals and plants live in shallow water along the coasts. Others live in the open sea a long way from land. A few living things even live in the deep sea, where it is dark and cold.

Where are the world's coldest habitats?

The world's coldest habitats are the Arctic and Antarctic. There, layers of ice and snow, called the polar ice caps, never melt. Few life forms can survive in this extreme cold. South of the Arctic ice cap is the tundra, where the ice melts each year, but the soil is always frozen.

DID YOU KNOW?
The dragon's blood tree grows only on the island of Socotra near Africa. The tree gets its name because, if scratched, it seeps red liquid like blood!

ABOVE In the summer, the tundra ice melts and a few plants grow. These include some flowering plants, such as poppies and heathers.

RIGHT A gibbon has long arms to help it swing through the trees.

How do animals survive?

Animals survive in their habitat by having special features to help them. For example, seals have a thick layer of fat to keep them warm in very cold water and some monkeys have long tails to hold onto branches. Some kinds of animals live in only one habitat. For example, squid only live in sea water. Other animals can live in two or more habitats. For example, mice live in fields, woodlands, and even in houses.

73

GRASSLAND HOMES

Why do grassland animals live in herds?

Some animals in the grasslands group together in herds to stay safe. This is because there are few trees and bushes to hide among in the wide open spaces of the grasslands. In a herd, most animals can have their heads down nibbling grass while others keep a lookout for danger. Grassland animals that form herds include elephants, zebras, and kangaroos.

How long is a giraffe's neck?

A giraffe's neck is nearly 8 feet long, which is longer than many surfboards. Giraffes use their long neck to reach the leaves on tall trees. This adaptation, or special feature, gives giraffes an advantage over grazing animals with shorter necks. This is vital in the grasslands, where there are many animals competing to eat the plant foods.

DID YOU KNOW?
Prairie dogs are not dogs at all. They are relatives of hamsters and live in groups of burrows called towns in the grasslands of North America.

Which is the fastest animal on land?

The fastest land animal in the world is the cheetah. It can sprint 325 feet in just over 3 seconds. It uses its speed to catch fast-running prey, such as antelopes. Other grassland predators catch prey in different ways. Lions creep up close to herds of wildebeest and zebra. They work in teams to chase, surround, and trap individuals, and then they share their meal.

What is a termite mound?

A termite mound is a nest made by antlike insects called termites. Termites live in hot grasslands in places such as Africa and Australia. Termite mounds are made from mud that sets hard in the heat. The mounds are up to 25 feet tall and inside there may be millions of termites. Air moving through tubes in the mounds keeps the termites cool.

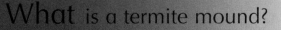

LEFT A large termite mound in Australia. Not all termites live in mounds. Some live in trees and others live underground.

SURVIVING IN A DESERT

Why don't cactus plants have leaves?

Plants lose water through their leaves when it is dry. Cactus plants live in dry deserts, so not having leaves helps them to save water. Instead of leaves, they have thick, green stems, which swell when their roots suck up water after short rain bursts. Cactuses also have spikes to stop animals from breaking into their stems to steal the precious water.

Which animal is called a thorny devil?

The thorny devil is a reptile that lives in the desert. It has an armor of spikes along its back to protect it from enemies. The thorny devil has an unusual way of getting the water it needs. When rain or dew lands on its back, the water flows along grooves leading to the corners of its mouth so that it can drink.

LEFT The thorny devil's spikes protect it from predators while it is busy hunting. It eats up to 3,000 ants a day.

How do fennec foxes use their big ears?

Like many desert animals, fennec foxes stay out of the sun because it is too hot. They are nocturnal, meaning they hunt at night and sleep during the day. The foxes use their huge ears to locate prey moving around in the dark. They have thick fur to keep them warm in the cold desert nights.

DID YOU KNOW?
Camels have eyelashes that are more than 4 inches long to stop the sand that blows around in desert storms from getting in their eyes.

RIGHT The fennec fox's hearing is sensitive enough to detect beetles, scorpions, and spiders scurrying over sand.

What do camels store in their humps?

Camels store fat in their humps to save for times when they cannot find enough food. The fat can be broken down to provide energy. When the fat is used up, the hump becomes droopy until the camel eats again. Camels can survive long periods without water, but after a drought, they can drink enough water in 10 minutes to fill a bathtub.

IN THE RAIN FOREST

Why do rain-forest trees grow so tall?

Rain-forest trees are tall because they
grow to reach the sunshine high up
in the forest canopy. The warmth and
moisture of rain-forest regions allows
the trees to grow quickly.

Rain-forest trees, such as teak, can
grow to up to 165 feet tall—or as high
as a lighthouse. Many different fruit and
nuts grow on the trees. These are eaten
by a great variety of animals.

Can frogs live in trees?

A flying frog

Yes, many different types of frog live in trees in the
rain forest. The frogs eat insects, and some lay
eggs in the tiny pools of water that form in the
leaves. One rain-forest frog, the flying frog,
glides across the gaps between the trees.
To do this, it stretches out the flaps of skin between its
toes like mini parachutes. Another tree frog is the
poison arrow frog. It has brightly colored skin to
warn predators that it is very poisonous and should
not be eaten.

Do plants ever grow on animals?

Yes, an animal called the sloth looks green because tiny plants called algae grow on its fur. Sloths live in the rain forests in South America, and the green color helps them to blend into the green leaves around them. Sloths crawl very slowly among branches using large, hooked claws. They eat leaves and fruit and only climb to the ground once a week to go to the bathroom.

DID YOU KNOW?
Leaf-cutter ants chew off pieces of rain-forest leaves and then carry them to their nest. They feed on the fungus that grows on the rotting leaves.

ABOVE Sloths sleep up to 18 hours a day, often hanging from branches. They spend most of their waking hours eating leaves.

How do forest-floor animals find food?

Some animals that live on the forest floor, such as agoutis, follow monkeys and parrots to find food. They gather the fruit and nuts that accidentally fall to the ground when the monkeys and parrots are feeding. Agoutis are relatives of guinea pigs and have big, strong front teeth. They use their teeth to gnaw open nuts that many other animals find too hard.

WOODLAND LIFE

HOW many leaves does an oak tree have?

A large oak tree grows about 250,000 new leaves each year in the spring. The leaves feed thousands of caterpillars and other insects. Animals, such as birds, feed on the insects. Oak, like beech and ash, is a deciduous woodland tree. This means that in the fall all its leaves fall to the ground, and the tree is bare over winter.

RIGHT Oak trees can live to be 1,000 years old or more. In the fall, their leaves turn a golden color.

Which woodland bird has a twisted beak?

The crossbill is a woodland bird that has a twisted, overlapping beak. The shape of the beak helps the bird to pluck seeds from inside the cones of conifer trees. Conifers are evergreen trees, which means that they have leaves all year. Their needle-shaped leaves are small and narrow to help reduce water loss in the cold, dry places where conifers mostly live.

Why do fallow deer have spotted backs?

Fallow deer have spotted backs to help them hide in the woods. The white spots look a little like the pattern made on the woodland floor by sunlight shining through gaps between the leaves. Patterns or coloring that help animals hide is called camouflage. Many other woodland animals use camouflage to avoid being seen by predators. For example, some moths look like tree bark and some caterpillars look like leaves.

Where do grizzly bears sleep in winter?

Grizzly bears sleep in winter in dens lined with twigs and grass. They dig their dens in sloping ground or may use a cave. The bears sleep all winter to save energy when there is not enough food. Some animals, such as snakes, go into a very deep sleep during winter called hibernation. They sleep so deeply that they appear to be dead.

MOUNTAIN LIFE

How do mountain plants survive the cold?

Plants survive on cold mountains in various ways. Most are small and grow in cracks among the rocks to keep out of the cold wind. The edelweiss traps warm air among hairs on its leaves and flowers. The alpine snowbell survives under snow during the winter. In spring, the dark color of its flowers absorbs enough heat from sunlight to melt the snow around them.

ABOVE Edelweiss has yellow flowers surrounded by hairy leaves.

What do giant pandas eat?

Giant pandas eat the stems and leaves of certain kinds of bamboo plant. The bamboo grows in forests on Chinese mountains. Giant pandas eat mainly bamboo, but they also eat insects and eggs that they find in the forest. The pandas feed on bamboo for up to 15 hours a day, eating about 45 pounds of the plant. Bamboo is a type of grass, which can grow up to 130 feet tall.

Which birds can fly higher than Mount Everest?

Vultures can fly higher than Mount Everest. They can reach heights of up to 7 miles, more than 1 mile higher than the world's highest mountain. Winds blowing up the mountain slopes help the birds to soar up high without having to flap their wings. Vultures are scavengers, meaning they eat animals that are already dead. They have good eyesight so they can see dead animals on the ground.

DID YOU KNOW?
African mountain gorillas have long, shaggy fur that enables them to stay warm in high mountain forests. The adults cannot climb the trees because they are so heavy they would break the branches.

BELOW Mountain goats have thick, fluffy hair to protect them from the cold.

How do mountain goats get a grip?

Mountain goats can grip the steep, rocky mountaintops because they have special hooves. The hooves have a soft, hollowed pad in the middle that acts a little like a sucker to grip the bare rocks. Using their hooves, mountain goats can run, jump, and climb across the rocks. They go to parts of the mountains where it would be too dangerous for predators, such as snow leopards, to follow.

LIFE IN THE FREEZER

Where do polar bears live?

Polar bears live in the Arctic, the region of the Earth around the icy North Pole. They feed mainly on seals and can hold their breath long enough to hunt seals underwater. Polar bears also catch food by finding the holes in the ice where the seals come to the surface for air. They then jump into the holes to grab their prey.

ABOVE Some people think polar bears eat penguins, but this is impossible because polars bears live at the North Pole and penguins live at the South Pole.

Why do Arctic foxes change color?

Arctic foxes change color to camouflage, or hide, themselves during the year. In winter, they have a white coat to stay hidden against the snow and ice. This helps the foxes to sneak up on prey. In summer, when the snow and ice have melted, the foxes grow a brown coat. Arctic foxes hunt lemmings, which are like voles, as well as birds. They also eat any seal meat left by

Do emperor penguins make nests?

No, emperor penguins do not make nests. In Antarctica, where they live, there are no twigs or pieces of plants to make nests from. Instead, the female lays one egg, which the male carries on top of his feet in a fold of blubbery skin. This keeps the egg warm it until hatches.

DID YOU KNOW?

In winter, people put a liquid called antifreeze in their cars to stop the water in their engines from freezing up. Antarctic cod produce their own special kind of antifreeze to stop their blood from freezing in icy waters.

ABOVE The emperor penguin is the largest penguin. The males can be up to 4 feet tall.

How do mammals keep warm in icy water?

Mammals that spend a lot of time in icy water keep warm by being very fat. Whales have a thick layer of blubber, or fat, under their skin, which can be up to 12 inches thick. Seals and sea lions have fur as well as blubber. This helps to keep them warm when they come onto the land to rest or to have their young.

Some whales feed on tiny shrimplike animals called krill, but they can live on their blubber when food is scarce.

WETLANDS AND LAKES

Which water plant has the biggest leaves?

The Amazon water lily has the biggest leaves. They are nearly 7 feet across and very strong. Plants that grow in wetlands and lakes have all the water they need, but they have to find clever ways of getting light for photosynthesis. Plants that grow in deep, dark water, such as water lilies, have floating leaves. Water lily leaves have air spaces inside that help them to float.

Do plants ever eat insects?

Yes, some plants catch insects for food. In bogs and swamps, the soil does not have enough of the substances that plants need to grow. Some carnivorous plants get these nutrients, or healthy substances, by trapping and digesting insects in different ways. The Venus flytrap has special leaves that open and shut like a book. When an insect lands on a Venus flytrap and touches tiny trigger hairs on its leaves, the leaves snap together, trapping the insect inside.

ABOVE The Venus flytrap's leaves are edged with spikes to stop the trapped insects from escaping.

Adult frog

Young frogs hop out of the water

Tadpoles grow legs

Eggs

Tadpoles

When do tadpoles become frogs?

Tadpoles become frogs when they are fully grown and it is time to live on land. Tadpoles hatch from eggs that frogs lay in the water. They have a long tail to swim with and look like fish. As the tadpoles turn into frogs, they increase in size and grow legs. Once they are frogs, they live on land, but they return to the water to lay their eggs.

Why do beavers build dams?

Beavers build dams across rivers to make deep ponds, then build their lodges, or homes, in the ponds. The dams and lodges are made of logs, mud, and rocks. The top of the lodge is above the water, but the entrance is deep underwater. This stops hunting predators, such as bears and wolves, from getting in. Inside, the lodge is warm and dry, and young beavers can live there in safety.

BELOW Beavers have thick fur to help keep them warm in cold water. They use their sharp teeth to cut the logs they need to build their dams and lodges.

DID YOU KNOW?
Wetlands are popular stopover places for migrating ducks and geese because there is a lot of water and food to eat.

LIVING IN RIVERS

Which trees grow by rivers?

Some trees, such as willow and alder, grow well in the damp soil by rivers. The trees use the river water to carry their floating seeds to new places, where the seeds may grow into trees. Tree roots in the soil help to stop the river banks from washing away. Animals, such as water voles and otters, often live in burrows among the tree roots.

RIGHT The branches of the weeping willow tree hang into the water.

BELOW Hippos use their big tusks to show off or even to fight each other.

What is a river horse?

A river horse is a hippopotamus. The name "hippopotamus" means "river horse" in ancient Greek. However, they are a distant relative of pigs and not horses. Hippos are big mammals that live in groups in African rivers. They wallow in shallow water and feed on grass. Their eyes, ears, and nostrils are on top of the head so that the rest of the head can stay underwater.

Can fish shoot their prey?

Some fish can shoot their prey. For example, the archer fish has an upturned mouth with a groove inside that it uses to squirt water at insects and other small animals. It knocks them into the water, where it can eat them. To keep other fish from getting the food once it has dropped in the river, the archer fish can also leap out of the water to grab its prey.

DID YOU KNOW?
The anaconda is the heaviest snake in the world. It can weigh 500 pounds and spends most of its time in rivers.

RIGHT An archer fish can shoot water up to 10 feet, but is most accurate when the prey is 3 feet or less away.

Why do crocodiles hide underwater?

Adult crocodiles hide in shallow river water to wait for animals that come to the edge to drink. Just their eyes are above the water, keeping a watch for prey. The crocodiles look out for thirsty birds, zebras, and even wildebeests. Then, they quickly burst out, grab the prey in their jaws, and drag it underwater to kill it.

COASTS AND CORAL REEFS

Does seaweed have roots?

Seaweed does not have roots because it does not need them. It gets its food from the water around it and not from soil like other plants. It uses parts called holdfasts to grip onto rocks to stop the tides and waves from washing it away. Many crabs and other invertebrates, such as limpets and starfish, eat seaweed.

ABOVE Seaweed grows mainly near coasts. It can be green, red, or brown.

Is coral dead or alive?

Coral is alive, but coral reefs are not. Coral polyps are tiny marine creatures that live in warm seas. To protect themselves from predators, or hunters, they produce stony skeletons. Over many years, the skeletons of millions of dead coral polyps slowly build up to form coral reefs. These reefs are important habitats for many kinds of fish.

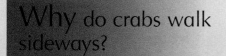

Why do crabs walk sideways?

Crabs walk sideways because their legs bend that way. Crabs have 10 legs, but they only use eight of them to move. The other two are claws. They use the claws to grasp food, fight other crabs, and to nip predators that get too close. A crab's flat shape and folding legs let it squeeze into holes to keep out of the way of predators.

DID YOU KNOW?
Sea otters catch seafood, such as clams, store them in their armpits, and then float on their backs while they dine.

When do sea turtles come ashore?

Sea turtles come ashore to lay their eggs on dry land. Turtles spend their lives at sea but, once a year, the females crawl up sandy beaches at night. They use their back flippers to dig holes, where they lay more than 100 eggs. The females bury the eggs and then swim away. When the baby turtles hatch, they make their way to the water.

OCEAN LIFE

BELOW The bottle-nosed dolphin's curved mouth makes it look like it is smiling.

How do dolphins hunt?

Dolphins hunt for fish in deep or dirty water using "echolocation." This means they make clicking noises and can tell where their prey is located by how the clicks echo, or bounce back. In clear waters, dolphins often hunt together in teams. They circle their prey and even chase it into shallow water to catch it.

Why does an octopus change color?

An octopus changes its color for camouflage, or to hide. It alters the color of its skin by squeezing tiny bags of ink under its skin. The octopus does this so it can blend in with the rock or sand nearby. Using this disguise, it can lie in wait to catch prey animals, such as lobsters, as they pass by.

What is an angler fish?

An angler fish is a type of fish that lives in the dark waters about half a mile below the ocean's surface. There, the only light comes from animals that make their own light. The angler fish has a glowing lure, like a fishing rod, dangling in front of its mouth. Any small fish that is attracted to the lure is grabbed in the angler fish's mouth.

LEFT The angler fish can open its mouth wide enough to swallow prey that is twice its size.

Can great white sharks smell blood?

Yes, great white sharks can smell blood from a long way away. This helps them find prey many miles away. Great white sharks eat mostly fur seals and sea lions. They can detect the blood in the water when seals and sea lions are giving birth. The sharks swim beneath their prey and catch them with their razor-sharp teeth.

LEFT Great white sharks have rows of jagged triangular teeth.

DID YOU KNOW?
The fangtooth is a vicious-looking deep-sea fish that has the largest teeth for its size in the ocean. Its teeth are so big, it cannot close its mouth fully!

ANIMALS UNDER THREAT

Which animals are under threat?

There are animals under threat in almost every habitat on Earth. This means that they are in danger of becoming extinct, or dying out. The main threat to wild animals is that people are damaging or destroying their habitats. When animals lose their homes, they have nowhere to live and no food. Some may be able to move to a new place, but many of them die.

RIGHT The snow leopard is under threat of extinction because it is hunted for its fur.

How are we destroying habitats?

People damage or destroy habitats in different ways. People cut down forests to make paper or to use the wood for building. People drain wetlands and dig up grasslands to make room for towns, factories, and airports. Some habitats are damaged by pollution. For example, rivers are damaged when factory waste or oil runs into them.

Why do people hunt elephants?

People hunt elephants to get their tusks, and then sell them to make carvings. Today, there are laws to try to stop people from hunting elephants, but many other animals are still threatened by hunters. For example, hunters kill rhinos and take their horns to be made into special knife handles. They also catch baby orangutans and chimpanzees and sell them as pets.

DID YOU KNOW?
To save the huge and almost extinct California condor, a zoo caught the last of these birds. It looked after them until their numbers increased and some could be released into the wild.

How can we save endangered animals?

People can help rhinos, elephants, and other animals under threat by joining conservation organizations. These are groups that raise money to help wild animals. They use the money to create nature reserves where wild animals can live safely. They also teach people about the dangers animals face and encourage people to help protect them.

95

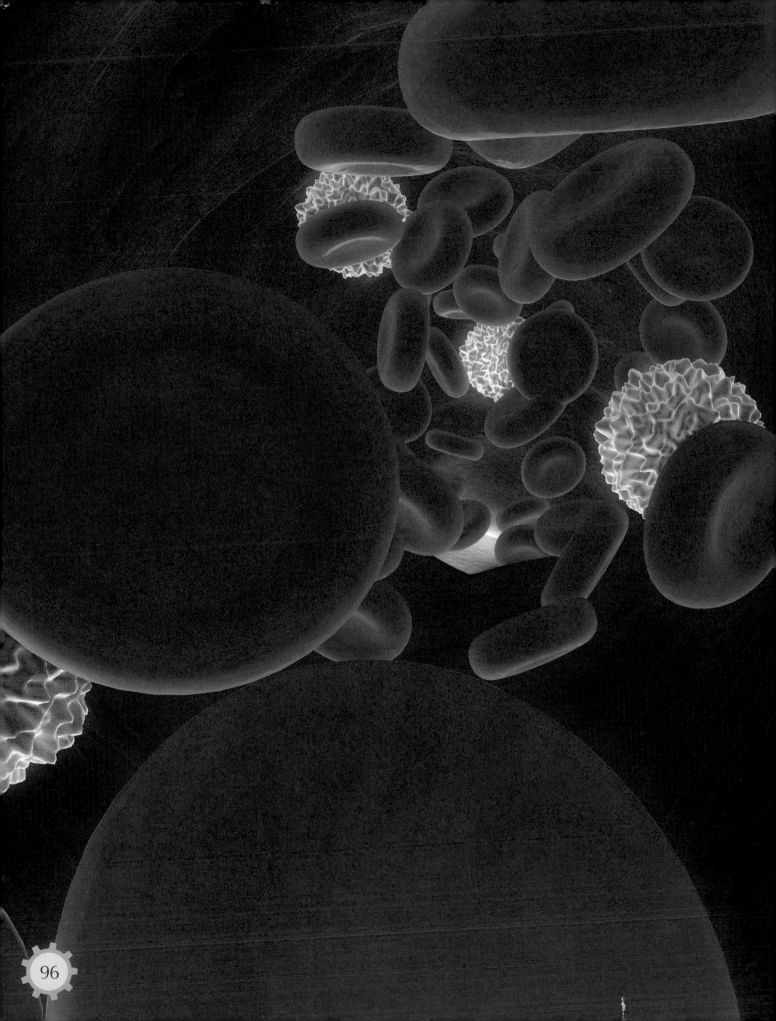

THE HUMAN BODY

Every moment of every day your body performs hundreds of tasks that keep you alive—your heart keeps beating, your lungs fill with air, food gets into your bloodstream, waste products are removed, and millions of electrical signals are sent to your brain. Your body even has the ability to replace parts when they wear out and heal itself when it becomes damaged. Most of this happens without you having to think about it.

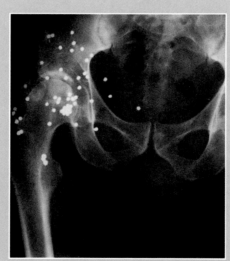

SKIN, NAILS, AND HAIR

BELOW Sweating helps keep our bodies cool in hot weather.

What is skin for?

Skin is for many different things. It acts like our body's armor, protecting the delicate parts inside our body from dirt, germs, and bumps. Skin also acts like a waterproof coat to keep out excess water, and it helps to keep us at the right temperature. Our skin gives us our sense of touch, so we can feel pain or tell whether something is hard or soft.

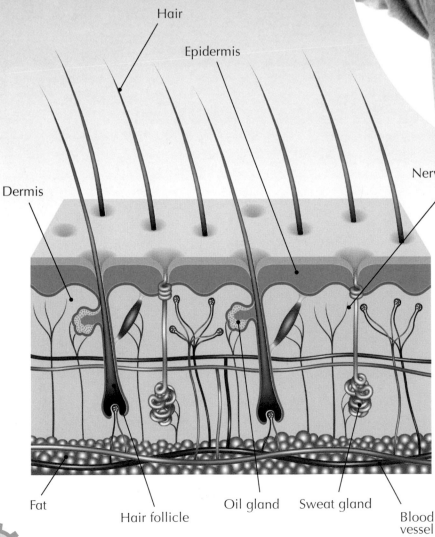

Hair

Epidermis

Nerve ending

Dermis

Fat

Hair follicle

Oil gland

Sweat gland

Blood vessel

What is skin made of?

Skin is made of three different layers. The top layer, or epidermis, contains a tough material called keratin, that makes your skin strong. The middle layer is called the dermis. It contains nerve endings that help you feel things, blood vessels that bring food and oxygen to the skin, and glands that make oil and sweat. The bottom layer is fat.

How long can nails grow?

Nails keep on growing and growing. If we don't cut our nails, they can become incredibly long. However, most people trim their nails to keep them short because nails have a useful job to do. Fingernails help us pick up, peel, and pluck things, and they protect our fingertips. It doesn't hurt when we cut our nails because they are made of keratin.

LEFT Our nails make our fingertips stronger and better at gripping objects.

BELOW Whether you have straight or curly hair, your hair does an important job. On a cold day, it keeps your head warm, and on a hot day, it protects your head from the sun.

DID YOU KNOW?
Altogether, a person has about 5 million hairs on their body—that is the same amount as a chimpanzee!

Why do some people have curly hair?

Some people have curly hair because of the type of hair follicle they have. The follicle is the place in the skin from which a hair grows. Round-shaped follicles make curly hair, while straight follicles make straight hair, and oval follicles make wavy hair. Next to each follicle is a gland that makes oil to keep your hair waterproof and shiny.

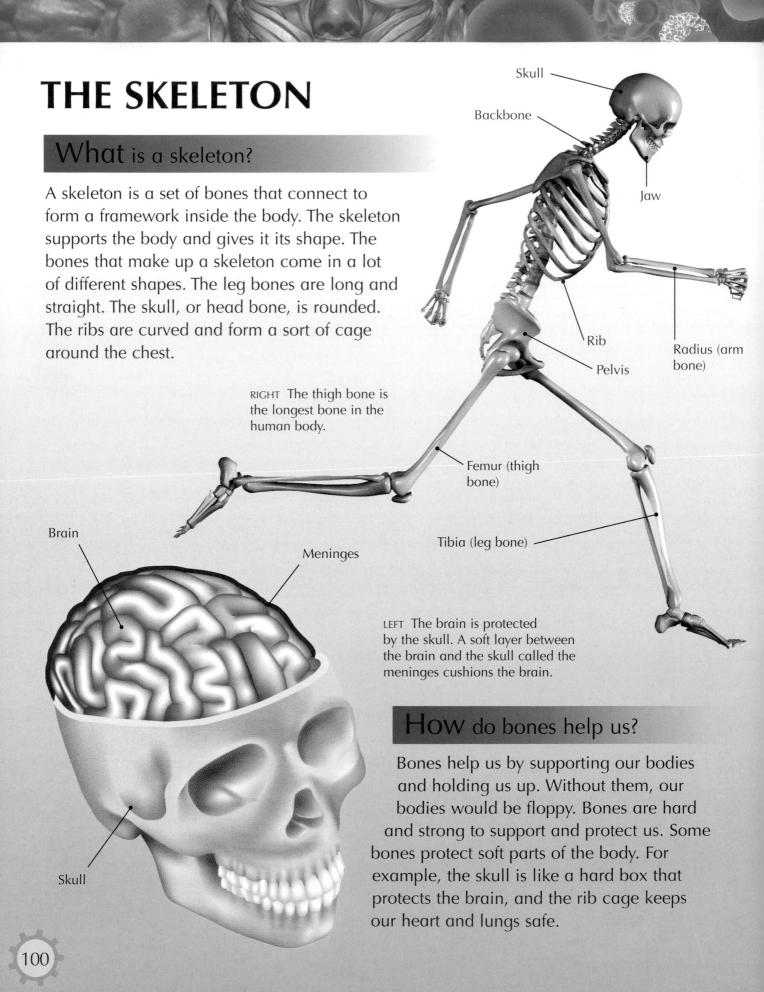

THE SKELETON

What is a skeleton?

A skeleton is a set of bones that connect to form a framework inside the body. The skeleton supports the body and gives it its shape. The bones that make up a skeleton come in a lot of different shapes. The leg bones are long and straight. The skull, or head bone, is rounded. The ribs are curved and form a sort of cage around the chest.

Skull

Backbone

Jaw

Rib

Pelvis

Radius (arm bone)

RIGHT The thigh bone is the longest bone in the human body.

Femur (thigh bone)

Tibia (leg bone)

Brain

Meninges

LEFT The brain is protected by the skull. A soft layer between the brain and the skull called the meninges cushions the brain.

Skull

How do bones help us?

Bones help us by supporting our bodies and holding us up. Without them, our bodies would be floppy. Bones are hard and strong to support and protect us. Some bones protect soft parts of the body. For example, the skull is like a hard box that protects the brain, and the rib cage keeps our heart and lungs safe.

100

Why do we need joints?

We need joints to move because bones are stiff and cannot bend. Joints are the places where bones meet. They connect different bones but also allow the bones to move. A hinge joint, such as the elbow, allows bones to move only one way. A ball-and-socket joint, such as the shoulder, allows movement in all directions—that is why you can swing your arms around.

RIGHT If a joint, such as the hip, becomes diseased, it may have to be replaced by an artificial joint. This X-ray shows a metal ball-and-socket hip.

When do bones grow?

Bones grow from before we are even born until we are about 20 years old. Bones are made of millions of tiny living cells and a mixture of hard substances that give bones their strength. The cells increase in number to make the bones grow. Even when people are fully grown, new cells form to replace old ones and to mend broken bones.

DID YOU KNOW?
There are over 200 different bones in an adult's body, and more than half of these are in the hands and feet.

LEFT A broken arm may need to be put in plaster and held in a sling until the bone mends.

101

MUSCLES AND MOVEMENT

Where are your muscles?

Your muscles are all over your body.
They are made of fibers bundled together,
which can get shorter to make a pulling
action. Most of your muscles make different
parts of your body move. These muscles
are attached to bones, and the bones
only move when your muscles pull them.
Your brain tells the muscles what to do.

RIGHT There are more than 600 muscles
in the human body, and they make up
about half of the body weight.

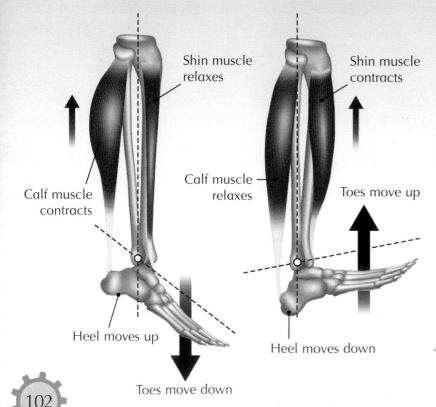

LEFT Lower and lift
your heel to see if you
can feel the muscles
in your lower leg
working in pairs.

Shin muscle
relaxes

Shin muscle
contracts

Calf muscle
relaxes

Calf muscle
contracts

Toes move up

Heel moves up

Heel moves down

Toes move down

How do muscles work?

Muscles work by pulling your bones.
They cannot push, so muscles have to
work in pairs. For example, in the lower
leg, the calf muscle contracts, or gets
shorter and harder, as it pulls on the
bone to lift the heel. At the same time,
the shin muscle on the front of the leg
relaxes, or stays long and soft. To reverse
the action, the shin muscle contracts,
pulling the toes up.

What are tendons?

Tendons are the rubbery ends of muscles that join muscles to bones. Tendons are a little like ropes. When you contract, or tighten, a muscle, the tendons move, and as they move, they pull the bones with them. The tendons in the hands connect to muscles in the arm that move the fingers.

BELOW You don't need muscles this big, but it is important to exercise to keep your muscles strong.

How do people get big muscles?

People get bigger, stronger muscles by doing exercise. Different activities exercise different muscles—cycling is good for leg muscles, while rowing gives arm muscles a workout. Stronger muscles are less likely to get damaged during exercise. They also have more stamina, which means they can keep going for longer without aching.

DID YOU KNOW?
Many of the muscles in your face are not attached to bone but to skin or each other. Working together, the tiny muscles move slightly to make you frown, smile, or wink.

THE BRAIN

How does your brain work?

Your brain works by sending and receiving messages through the nerves in your body. The nerves act like the body's telephone system. Information from your senses passes along nerves, up the spinal cord (a long nerve inside your backbone), all the way to your brain. Your brain can store this information and use it to send a message back to the body.

BELOW When you touch something, nerves send a message to the brain. The brain works out what the message means and sends a message back.

Brain

Spinal cord

Nerves

When do you feel pain?

You feel pain when your brain tells you to. When you touch something sharp or hot, nerves in your fingertips send a message to your brain to warn it of the danger. The brain processes this information and tells the muscles in your arm to move your hand away from the source of pain as quickly as possible.

Touch, movement

Feelings, personality, behavior

Sight

Language, speech, hearing

What does your brain do?

Your brain controls your body. It tells the rest of your body what to do and when to do it. Different parts of the brain have different jobs. The biggest part is the cerebrum, and it does most of the thinking based on information it gets from your senses. The right half of your brain controls the left side of your body, and the left half controls the right side.

ABOVE Different parts of the cerebrum work different parts of the body. These are just a few of its functions.

DID YOU KNOW?
Messages traveling along the spinal cord to the brain race along at over 180 miles an hour—which is faster than most high-speed trains.

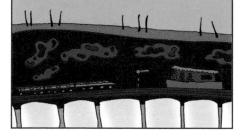

Does your brain ever rest?

No, even when you are in a deep sleep your brain never rests. The brain is always on the go. At night, it keeps your heart beating, makes sure you breathe, and controls many other body functions. This is also the time when the brain processes, or sorts out, all the new stuff you learned during the day.

EYES AND SIGHT

How do eyes work?

Your eyes work by taking pictures of the world and sending them to your brain. Light from an object passes through the lens in the middle of your eye. The lens focuses the light onto the retina at the back of the eye. The retina changes light patterns into signals that it sends to the brain. The brain changes the signals into a picture to tell you what your eyes are seeing.

BELOW The iris controls the size of the pupil, which is the space that lets in light. In the dark, the pupil dilates, becoming very big, to let in as much light as possible.

Blood vessels

Optic nerve to brain

Pupil

Cornea

Iris

Lens

Retina

Vitreus humor (the liquid that fills the eyeball)

BELOW When you look at an object in front of you, each eye sees it from a slightly different angle. The brain combines the images from these two angles into a single three-dimensional image.

Why do we need two eyes?

We need two eyes because together they help us see things properly. Each eye gives the brain a slightly different view of something, and the brain uses those little differences to work out exactly how far away the object is. This is called depth perception. Having depth perception helps us do things, such as catch a ball, shake hands, or pick up a pin.

What is an optical illusion?

An optical illusion is a picture that tricks us into thinking we can see something that is not really there or is impossible. The brain tries to make sense of the picture. For example, a Necker cube is just a drawing of lines on a page, but the brain tries to make sense of it. The brain tells you it is a cube, even though it is an impossible cube!

RIGHT Although the dots in the middle of each of these two groups of dots are the same size, the brain is tricked into thinking they are different sizes.

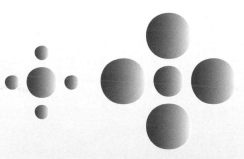

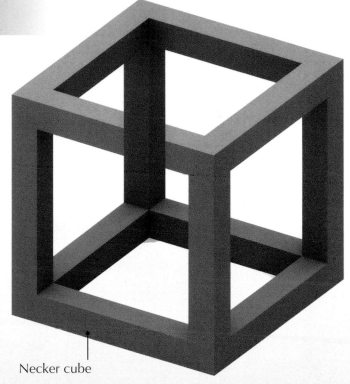

Necker cube

DID YOU KNOW?
The average person blinks between 10,000 and 20,000 times every day. A blink is so quick that it only takes about a tenth of a second.

When do you blink?

You usually blink once every five seconds. You may not even notice you are doing it. Blinking keeps your eyes clean and moist. When you blink, your eyelid spreads tears over the front of the eye. This stops the eyes from drying out and washes out pieces of dirt and dust. Blinking also helps to stop dust and dirt from getting into your eyes in the first place.

LEFT When you cry, your eyes produce tears. Tears are mostly water, but they also contain substances that kill germs.

EARS, HEARING, AND BALANCE

Semicircular canals

Ossicles

Eardrum

Nerve

Cochlea

Outer ear

What happens inside your ears?

A process takes place inside your ears, which turns sounds into signals to the brain. Sounds make the air vibrate, or move to and fro, and the vibrating air makes the eardrum vibrate. The eardrum is joined to a set of tiny bones, called ossicles, so they vibrate, too. The ossicles pass the vibrations to a tube called the cochlea. When tiny hairs inside the cochlea move, they send signals along a nerve to the brain.

Why do you have two ears?

You have two ears because one ear on each side of your head helps you work out where sounds are coming from. For example, before crossing a road, you look and listen for cars. The sound of a car reaches one ear before the other. Your brain uses the slight difference to judge how far away the car is and check if it is safe to cross.

RIGHT Headphones send music to both ears, making it sound more like you are hearing it live.

108

How do gymnasts balance?

Gymnasts balance using their ears. Inside the ear, there are three bony tubes called semicircular canals that are filled with fluid. When the body moves, so does the fluid in these tubes. The brain uses these slight changes to sense even the smallest movement. This allows a gymnast to adjust her arms or legs in order to keep her balance.

DID YOU KNOW?
When you get off a merry-go-round, you feel dizzy because the fluid in your semicircular canals keeps moving for a few moments after you stop turning.

RIGHT Bats make very high-pitched noises that humans cannot hear.

RIGHT Gymnasts use their sense of balance to help them do handstands and other difficult moves.

Which sounds can you hear?

You can hear a lot of sounds but not all of the sounds in the world. For example, people cannot hear the sounds bats make or many of the noises underwater animals make to communicate with each other. The sounds that people hear most clearly are other people's voices. That is because being able to hear other people is an important form of communication for us.

109

BREATHING, TALKING, AND SMELLING

What is breathing?

Breathing is moving air into and out of the body. You breathe in because you need oxygen from the air. You take in air through your nose and mouth and into your lungs. Oxygen passes from the lungs into the blood, which carries it around your body. When you breathe out, you get rid of the waste gas, carbon dioxide.

RIGHT We need to breathe all the time, but we cannot breathe underwater. Divers have to take tanks of oxygen with them to breathe from.

How do lungs work?

Lungs work by sucking air in and forcing air out. When you inhale, or breathe in, the lungs get bigger. To give your lungs room, muscles in your chest pull your ribs upward and outward. A sheet of muscle just below the lungs, called the diaphragm, is pulled downward. When you exhale, or breathe out, your ribs fall back and the diaphragm relaxes again.

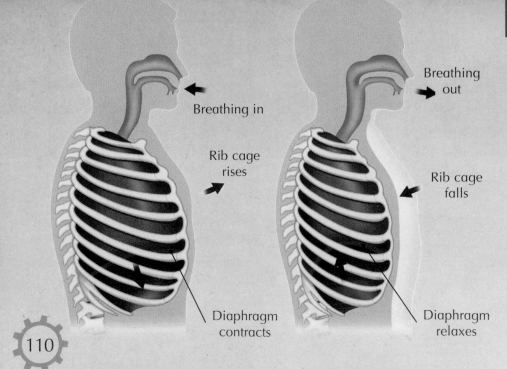

Breathing in

Rib cage rises

Diaphragm contracts

Breathing out

Rib cage falls

Diaphragm relaxes

Why do you talk through your mouth?

You talk through your mouth because you use the air that you breathe out to make sounds. When you talk, air from your lungs passes over flaps of skin in your neck called vocal cords. The moving air makes the vocal cords vibrate, and this produces sounds.

You turn the sounds into words by changing the shape of your mouth and tongue.

DID YOU KNOW?
When you sneeze to get rid of unwanted pieces of dirt and dust up your nose, air comes out of your nostrils at about 100 miles an hour—that is faster than cars on a highway.

How do you smell things?

You smell things when you breathe in and air passes through your nose. The inside of your nose is lined with nerve cells that sense odors in the air. The nerves send messages to the brain, which then works out what the smells are. Your sense of smell is important. It can warn you of danger— for example, if you smell smoke from a fire.

111

HEART AND BLOOD

Why does your heart beat?

Your heart beats so that it can pump blood around your body. The heart is an organ in the middle of your chest, and it is partly made up of muscles. As its muscles contract, or tighten, the heart pushes blood around the blood vessels, or tubes, inside your body. The blood carries digested food and oxygen around the body and takes away waste.

Artery (blood vessel that takes blood from the heart around the body)

Heart

Vein (blood vessel that returns blood to the heart)

LEFT A doctor can hear your heart beating by listening to it with a stethoscope.

Where does blood go?

Blood goes all around the body and back again. After it leaves the heart, the blood delivers oxygen to the body. By the time the blood returns to the heart, the oxygen has been used up. So, the heart sends the blood to the lungs to collect more oxygen. Then, it passes back to the heart to be pumped around the body again.

ABOVE Each time your heart beats, a wave of blood is pushed along a blood vessel running from the heart.

112

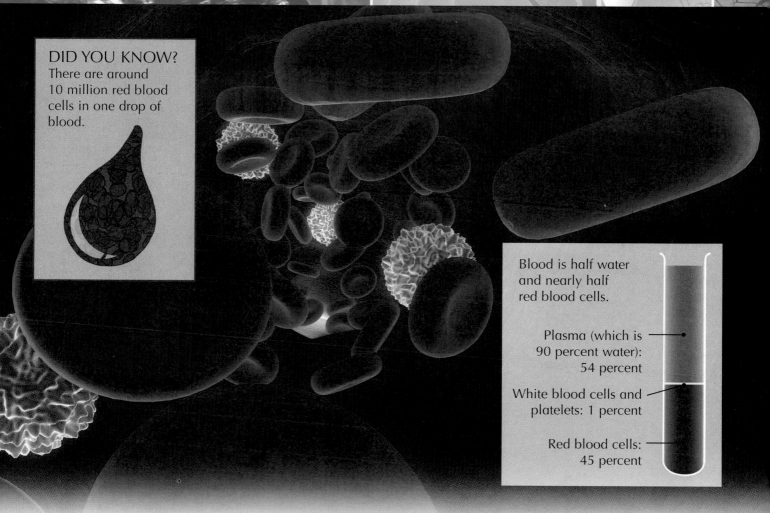

DID YOU KNOW?
There are around 10 million red blood cells in one drop of blood.

Blood is half water and nearly half red blood cells.

Plasma (which is 90 percent water): 54 percent

White blood cells and platelets: 1 percent

Red blood cells: 45 percent

BELOW Because our bodies can make new blood, people can donate some of their blood to save the life of someone who has lost a lot of blood.

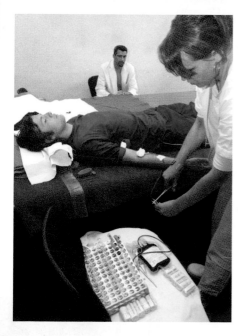

Why is blood red?

Blood is red because there are red blood cells in it. Red cells contain hemoglobin, a chemical that carries oxygen, and this is what makes them red. Blood contains a fluid called plasma, plus red blood cells, white blood cells, and platelets. White blood cells fight harmful germs. Platelets stop us from bleeding to death when our skin is cut by clotting (setting) the blood.

How much blood do you have?

An adult has between 8 and 13 pints of blood. When old blood cells wear out, new ones are made inside your bones in the part called the bone marrow. We each have one of eight different types of blood, called blood groups. If someone loses blood in an accident, doctors are careful to check which blood group is needed before giving them new blood.

GETTING SICK

Where do germs come from?

Germs come from the world around us. These tiny living things are found in the air, in soil, in water, and sometimes in food. Germs can make you sick if they get inside your body through openings, such as the mouth, nose, or a cut in the skin. They can cause diseases, such as colds and the flu.

BELOW Scientists look at germs by magnifying them many times under a microscope.

ABOVE Someone who has a cold should use a handkerchief when sneezing. Otherwise, the cold germs get into the air.

How do germs make you sick?

Germs make you sick because they start living inside your body. Your body is made up of millions of tiny parts called cells. To live inside you, germs take energy and food from your body's cells. This leaves your body feeling weaker. Germs also produce waste, and when the waste gets into your system, it can make you very sick.

Can your body fight disease?

Yes, your body can often fight disease. When germs get inside you, white blood cells in your blood start to make antibodies. These are special chemicals that find germs and then stick to them. This helps other white blood cells in your blood locate the germs and try to destroy them. When you are sick, your body makes more white blood cells to protect you.

Antibodies stick to the germ.

Germ

White blood cell destroys the germ.

ABOVE The antibodies help the white blood cell to recognize the germ so it can destroy it.

What are vaccinations?

Vaccinations are injections of a special medicine called a vaccine. Vaccines can prevent you from catching some serious diseases. A vaccine contains a harmless amount of a particular disease. When the vaccine is inside you, your body makes antibodies to attack it. These antibodies stay in your blood for a long time. If you ever catch the disease, they are ready and waiting to help destroy it.

BELOW Most vaccines are given by injections such as this one.

DID YOU KNOW?
A bar of soap can protect you from disease. Washing your hands gets rid of germs picked up from things you have touched.

TASTE AND EATING

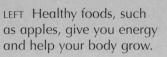

LEFT Healthy foods, such as apples, give you energy and help your body grow.

Why do you need to eat?

You need to eat because food is the body's fuel. The body breaks food down in a process called digestion, releasing the materials your body needs. Your body is made up of millions of tiny cells. These cells use energy from digested food to make new cells so you can grow or to replace old cells. Some food also supplies the materials needed to build body parts, such as muscles.

How do you taste food?

You taste food using your tongue and your nose. Your tongue is covered with taste buds that sense different flavors in food and send signals to the brain. Your nasal (nose) tubes run into your mouth, and the smell of the food in your mouth also helps your brain decide what it tastes like.

RIGHT It was long believed that four tastes were sensed in different parts of the tongue. Scientists now think that there are five tastes, which can be sensed across the whole tongue.

Bitter

Sour

Sour

Sweet

Salty

Sharp front tooth

Top row of teeth

Flat-topped back tooth

Bottom row of teeth

ABOVE Your top and bottom teeth work together to cut and mash food.

What happens when you chew food?

When you chew food, your teeth break it down so your body can digest it. The teeth cut the food into small pieces and the saliva (spit) in your mouth makes it soft. Your teeth are different shapes to do different jobs. The front teeth bite and slice, while the back teeth chew and mash the food.

DID YOU KNOW?
The process of digestion starts even before you eat. As soon as you smell food, your mouth makes saliva, ready to soften the food when it is in your mouth.

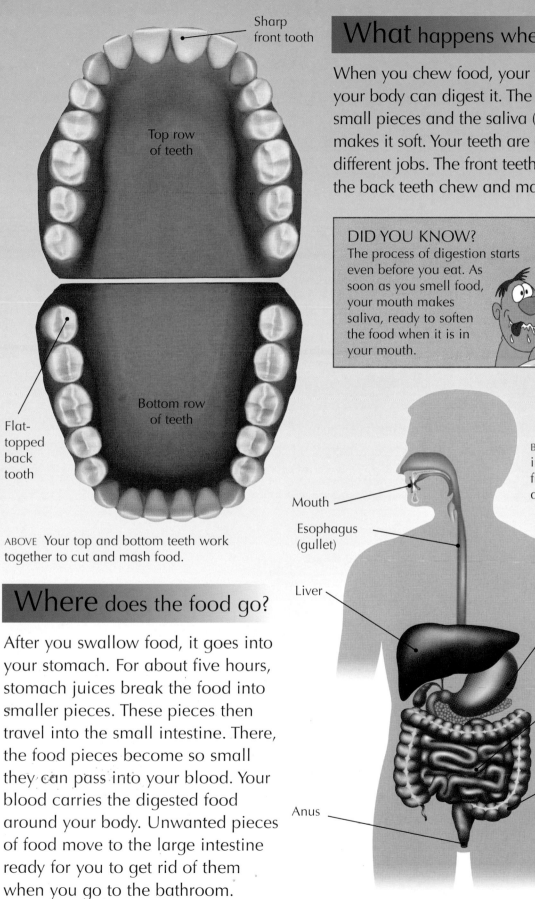

BELOW Food is digested in a long tube that runs from the mouth to the anus (rear end).

Mouth

Esophagus (gullet)

Liver

Anus

Stomach

Small intestine

Large intestine

Where does the food go?

After you swallow food, it goes into your stomach. For about five hours, stomach juices break the food into smaller pieces. These pieces then travel into the small intestine. There, the food pieces become so small they can pass into your blood. Your blood carries the digested food around your body. Unwanted pieces of food move to the large intestine ready for you to get rid of them when you go to the bathroom.

117

VITAL ORGANS

Where is your liver?

Your liver is found below your ribs on the right of your body. It is a part of the body called an organ. Your organs all have important jobs to do. The liver does a number of different jobs. For example, it filters, or removes, harmful substances from the blood. It stores nutrients, such as vitamins and iron, for the body. It also helps you digest food by producing bile, a juice that breaks down food in the stomach.

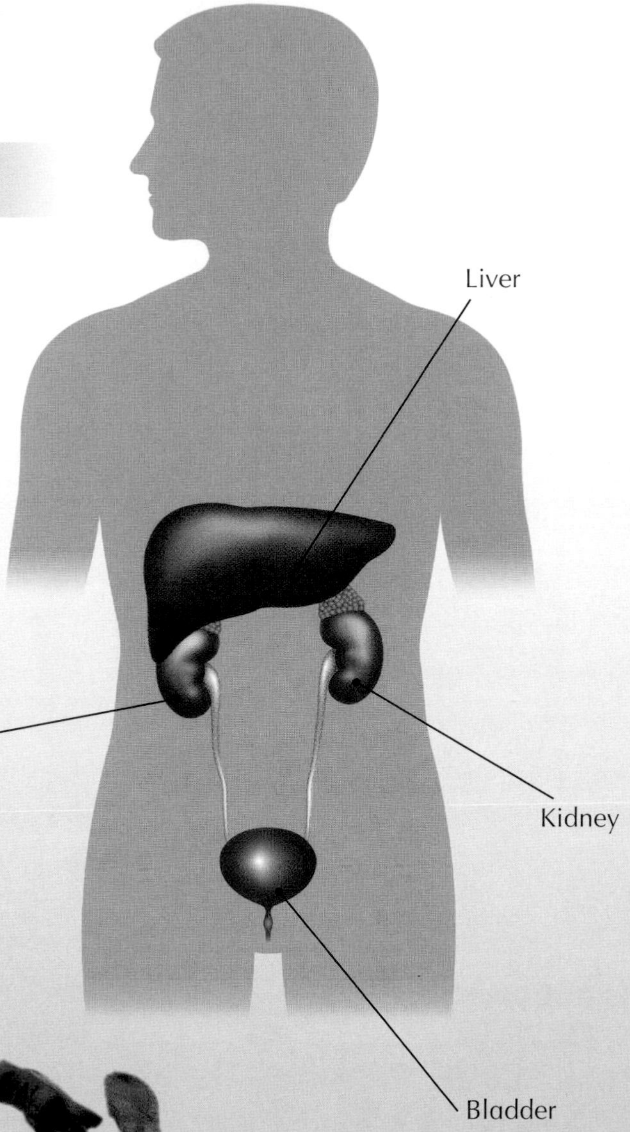

Liver

Kidney

Kidney

RIGHT The liver is the largest organ in the body. This picture shows you where it is located in relation to other important organs, such as the bladder and kidneys.

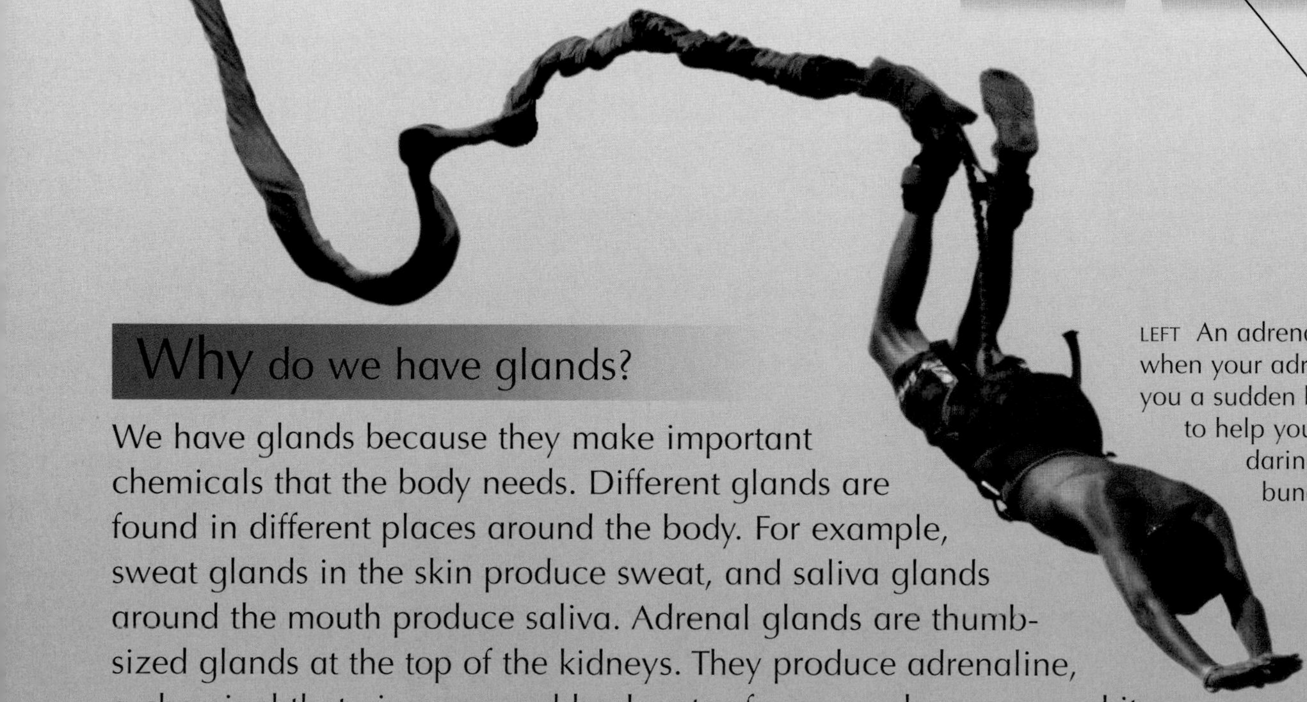

Bladder

Why do we have glands?

We have glands because they make important chemicals that the body needs. Different glands are found in different places around the body. For example, sweat glands in the skin produce sweat, and saliva glands around the mouth produce saliva. Adrenal glands are thumb-sized glands at the top of the kidneys. They produce adrenaline, a chemical that gives you sudden bursts of energy when you need it.

LEFT An adrenaline rush is when your adrenal glands give you a sudden burst of energy to help you do something daring, such as a bungee jump.

How do we get rid of waste?

We get rid of waste using our kidneys. As the blood circulates around our body, one of the blood's jobs is to collect waste from the body's cells. If this waste were to build up in our body, it would poison us. When blood passes through the kidneys, the kidneys remove the waste and collect it in urine. Urine is stored in the bladder until we are ready to go to the bathroom.

BELOW Our kidneys need water to function properly.

DID YOU KNOW?
The pituitary gland is only the size of a pea, but it produces important chemicals that control growth. Sometimes, it produces too much and people grow very tall.

What is a kidney transplant?

A kidney transplant is an operation in which a person whose kidneys have failed gets a new kidney. People can live a normal life with only one kidney, so sometimes a relative will donate one of their kidneys to a family member who needs one. In a kidney-transplant operation, a person's old kidneys are left in place and a new kidney is placed lower down.

A NEW LIFE

HOW is a baby made?

A baby is made when two very tiny cells, one from a father and one from a mother, join together. The male cell is called a sperm and the female cell is called an egg. The cells are so tiny, you can only see them under a microscope. After they join, they begin to grow and a baby develops.

ABOVE Sperms look similar to little tadpoles. Only one will join the mother's egg.

HOW does a baby grow?

A baby grows when a new cell forms from the sperm and egg cells. This new cell is called a zygote. The zygote then divides into two. Then these two cells divide. This process is called cell division. It goes on and on, and as new cells form, they gather together in different groups to make different parts of the baby's body.

RIGHT The zygote divides many times in the mother's womb as it grows into a baby.

When is a baby ready to be born?

A baby grows inside its mother for a total of nine months before it is ready to be born. At first, it is very small. After three months, it is still only about three inches long, although it already has hands, feet, eyes, a nose, and a mouth. By the time it is born, a baby is much bigger, but it is still helpless and needs to be fed and cared for.

LEFT An ultrasound scan shows a baby inside its mother.

DID YOU KNOW?

A baby can cry as soon as it is born. Crying does not necessarily mean a baby is unhappy, but it is the only way a baby can tell people what it needs.

Why do children look like their parents?

Children look like their parents because of their genes. Genes are a special kind of instruction code found in the cells in the body. Genes tell the cells what kind of cell they should turn into. They are passed on from a mother and father when a baby is made. That is why children often look a little like their parents.

GROWING UP

How fast do babies grow?

Babies grow and change at an incredible rate in the first year of their life. By the age of one, a baby is usually three times heavier than it was when it was born, and it changes in other ways, too. By four months old, a baby can sit propped up, smile, and hold toys. By a year old, a baby can stand and maybe even walk and say a few simple words.

How do children change?

Children change, learn and develop in a lot of ways as they get older. In addition to getting taller and looking older, children learn to read and write, take care of themselves, and learn new skills, such as riding a bike. Children learn a lot by playing but also by watching and copying other people and listening carefully to what they say.

BELOW Reading is one of the skills that children learn as they grow.

DID YOU KNOW?
Children grow fastest in the first two years of life and during puberty. As teenagers, boys can grow by four inches a year and girls by three inches a year.

What is puberty?

Puberty is the time in your life when your body begins to change and develop. You become an adult instead of a child. Puberty can begin any time between 8 and 14 years old. One of the signs of puberty is that you suddenly start to grow taller. Girls grow into a more womanly shape, and boys find that their voices get deeper and hair grows on their faces.

LEFT During their teenage years, children start to feel and act more like adults.

When do people stop growing?

People stop growing after puberty, when they become adults. This is usually when they are about 18 to 20 years old. At this time, bones stop getting longer and people reach their full height.

RIGHT After about 20 years old, we slowly start to age because some of our worn-out cells are not replaced by the body.

123

KEEPING HEALTHY

What should you eat?

You should eat a mixture of different kinds of food to keep healthy. You should try to include a carbohydrate, such as pasta, rice, or bread, at every meal and eat at least five different fruit and vegetables each day. You also need a small amount of protein, such as cheese or meat, two or three times a day. Fats, oils, and sugars are useful foods, but you should only eat small amounts of these.

LEFT A food pyramid shows you how much you can eat of different foods. The foods at the bottom of the pyramid are those that you can eat the most of. The foods at the top should only be eaten for a special treat.

About two-thirds of the body is water.

DID YOU KNOW?
Eating carrots really can help our eyesight. Carrots and other foods, such as apricots, milk, and asparagus, contain a lot of vitamin A, which helps us see.

Why is water good for you?

Water is good for you because your body needs water to work properly. There is water in your brain, blood, joints, and many other places. You lose water every day, for example, through sweating or going to the bathroom. You need to take in more water to make up for this loss. You can do this by drinking water and eating foods that contain water, such as fruit, vegetables, and soup.

How does exercise help?

Exercise helps in many different ways. It makes your growing bones and muscles strong. Exercise that makes you breathe harder, such as cycling, also strengthens your heart and lungs. Exercise makes you feel in better shape and helps you to relax and sleep better. It can also make you feel happier, and it is a good way to make new friends. It does not matter what kind of exercise you do, as long as you enjoy it.

RIGHT Swimming is an excellent form of exercise. It keeps your heart and lungs healthy and also helps strengthen your muscles and bones.

When should you go to bed?

When you should go to bed depends on how much sleep you need. Babies need to sleep up to 16 hours a day, but old people may need only about 6 hours' sleep. Most children need at least 10 hours' sleep to keep healthy. When you sleep, your body rests and your brain sorts through the new information you have taken in during the day.

LEFT Getting enough sleep is important for you to feel healthy and to have energy to do things.

125

WORLD HISTORY

Humans first appeared on the Earth around 200,000 years ago. Since then, people have changed the world they live in. They have settled all over the planet, developed language and writing, invented amazing machines, and even explored space. Human history is full of bloody wars and brutal conquests, but there have also been wonderful achievements in art, science, medicine, and many other areas. History may be the story of the past, but it also helps us understand the present and the future.

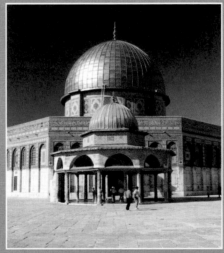

ANCIENT EGYPT

When were the pyramids built?

The ancient Egyptians first built pyramids over 4,500 years ago. They built them as tombs for their rulers, who were called pharaohs. After a pharaoh died, the ruler's precious belongings were buried in the pyramid so they could be used in the afterlife. The ancient Egyptians ruled a vast area of north Africa from about 5,000 years ago until Egypt became part of the Roman Empire in 30 BC.

ABOVE Pyramids were built using thousands of stone blocks that were brought by boat along the Nile River.

How were mummies made?

In ancient Egypt, the first step in making a mummy was to remove the liver, lungs, and other organs from inside the dead body. Then the body was covered in a kind of salt to dry it out. After 40 days, the body was oiled to stop the skin from cracking. The body was stuffed and then wrapped in cloth. Finally, it was sealed inside a coffin called a sarcophagus.

LEFT Mummification has preserved the bodies of ancient Egyptians for more than 5,000 years.

What are hieroglyphics?

Hieroglyphics are a special kind of picture writing that was used by the ancient Egyptians. Hieroglyphics are found on temples and tomb walls and on rolls of papyrus. Papyrus was a kind of paper made from a reed plant that grew along the banks of the Nile. A lot of what we know about ancient Egypt comes from these hieroglyphic writings.

Why was the Nile River important?

Without the Nile River, ancient Egypt would not have become so rich and powerful. Every year the river flooded and water spilled onto the desert. This made the soil good for growing many food plants. Farmers also dug channels from the river to water fields farther away. The ancient Egyptians caught fish from the river and traded goods up and down it by boat.

BELOW Hieroglyphics were either carved into walls or painted onto rolls of papyrus.

ANCIENT GREECE

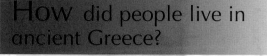

How did people live in ancient Greece?

Life in ancient Greece was different for men and women and for rich and poor. Greek men ran the government of their cities and were often away from home fighting wars. Women ran things at home but rarely left the house. Most Greek families owned slaves, who did all the household chores and manual labor, but had no rights or freedom.

ABOVE The Greeks depicted their lives and those of their gods in wonderful carvings.

What happened in Greek temples?

In the temples, priests watched over statues of the Greek gods and goddesses, while ordinary people worshipped the gods outside the temple. The Greeks built statues and temples to keep their gods happy because they believed that the gods behaved just like people, even having arguments, fights, and parties. If the gods were happy, they would help and look after the Greek people.

LEFT The Parthenon in Athens is the most famous Greek temple of all. It was built 2,500 years ago.

130

When were the first Olympic Games?

The Olympic Games began 2,700 years ago. At first, the Games were a religious festival held in honor of Zeus, the king of the Gods, and the only athletic event was a short sprint. However, sports were important to the Greeks and, gradually, more competitions were added. Eventually, the Olympic Games became a five-day festival held every four years, which people from all over the ancient Greek world came to see.

BELOW The discus was one of the events at the earliest Olympic Games.

Who acted at Greek theatres?

Early Greek plays had only one actor, plus a group of performers, called the chorus, who chanted and sang. Later plays had more parts, but they were all were played by men—even the female characters. Greek theaters were built outside with stone, steplike seats cut into hillsides. Many of these open-air theaters were big enough to hold up to 10,000 people.

BELOW Greek theaters were so well designed that even the people at the back could hear the actors on stage.

DID YOU KNOW?
The lost city of Atlantis is believed to have been an ancient Greek city that disappeared under the sea following an enormous volcanic eruption.

ANCIENT ROMANS

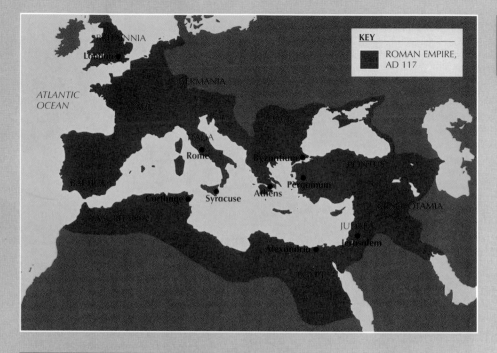

KEY

ROMAN EMPIRE, AD 117

BRITANNIA
London
ATLANTIC OCEAN
GERMANIA
GAUL
DACIA
ITALIA
Rome
Byzantium
PONTUS
BAETICA
Carthage
Syracuse
Athens
Pergamum
MESOPOTAMIA
MAURETANIA
JUDAEA
Alexandria
Jerusalem
EGYPT

How big was the Roman Empire?

At its biggest, the Roman Empire included lands stretching from Britain to North Africa and from Spain to the Middle East. The emperor ruled the empire from the capital city, Rome, in what is now Italy. The empire was biggest in the second century AD, during the reign of Emperor Trajan.

Which weapons did Roman soldiers fight with?

A Roman soldier's weapons included a spear for throwing at the enemy and a short sword. Roman soldiers were well trained and fought as a team. To defend themselves against attack from arrows, some soldiers would hold their shields over their heads like a roof to protect the group.

BELOW Roman soldiers wore heavy body armor and iron helmets which protected the face and head.

Who were the gladiators?

Gladiators were slaves who were trained to fight in order to entertain audiences in an amphitheater. Gladiators had to fight each other as well as wild animals, such as lions or bears. When one of the gladiators lost a fight, sometimes the audience decided if he would live or die. Successful gladiators were often rich and famous.

What did the Romans build?

The Romans built well-planned cities and towns with beautiful stone buildings. They constructed aqueducts, or channels, to bring water from distant mountain springs to their cities. They excavated underground drains to take waste away from their cities, and they built the first apartment buildings, bath houses, and amphitheaters, such as the Colosseum.

BELOW The Colosseum in Rome held about 50,000 people, who came to be entertained by the gladiator fights.

DID YOU KNOW?
The Circus Maximus in Rome was a huge stadium for horse and chariot racing. It was 1,870 feet long and 460 feet wide and could hold up to 250,000 people—one-quarter of the people of Rome!

THE VIKINGS

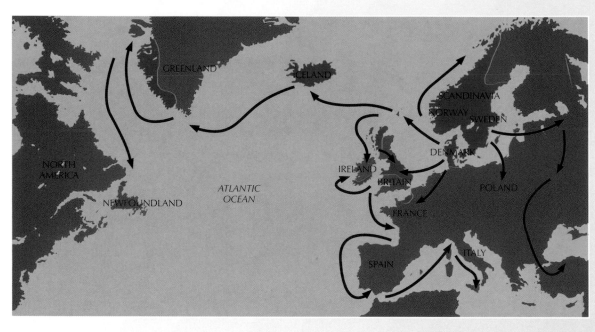

GREENLAND

ICELAND

SCANDINAVIA
NORWAY
SWEDEN

NORTH AMERICA

DENMARK

IRELAND

NEWFOUNDLAND

ATLANTIC OCEAN

BRITAIN

POLAND

FRANCE

SPAIN

ITALY

LEFT This map shows the areas where the Vikings settled. The Vikings even reached North America, settling in Newfoundland around AD 1000.

Where did the Vikings come from?

The Vikings came from the area we now call Scandinavia in around AD 800. Many of them were farmers and hunters. Their families lived in a long, single-roomed wooden hall and cooked on an open fire in the middle of the hall. The Vikings were skilled craftspeople, making pots and pans, silver and gold jewelry, and bronze tools and weapons.

Why did Vikings raid other places?

Vikings left home to raid, or steal from, other lands because there was not enough farmland for everybody in their homeland. Many Vikings sailed on wooden ships to steal goods, such as gold crosses and holy books covered with jewels. They also attacked villages and farms and kidnapped people to work as slaves.

What were Viking ships like?

Viking raiding ships were long and narrow with a large, square sail. They could move quickly through the water, and they were strong enough to cope with rough seas and long voyages. Some boats carried 200 fighting men. The boats would land right on the beach so that Viking warriors could leap straight out to attack any local people trying to defend their land.

DID YOU KNOW?
In addition to raiding, the Vikings also traveled far and wide. They bought and sold goods, bringing back furs from Iceland and silk and spices from the Middle East.

LEFT The chief Viking god, Odin, was the god of war, wisdom, poetry, and the dead.

Who did the Vikings worship?

The Vikings worshipped many gods. These included Thor, the god who threw his hammer when angry and created thunder and storms. Freya, the goddess of love, wept tears of gold. The stories they told about their gods are known as Norse myths. The English word "Thursday" comes from the god Thor's name and "Friday" comes from the name Freya.

135

AZTECS, INCAS, AND MAYA

Why did the Maya build pyramids?

The ancient Maya people built tall, step-sided pyramids
to act as temples. These temples were decorated
with pictures of their main gods—the Sun, Moon,
Earth, and rain gods. On top of the temples were
observatories to study the stars. The Maya controlled
an empire across Mexico and Central America
between AD 200 and 1550.

BELOW The top Aztec warriors
carried wooden clubs with sharp
stone blades along the sides.

Who were the Aztecs?

The Aztecs were hunters who settled in Mexico
in around 1200. Aztec warriors took over
other lands and soon their empire included 12
million people. At the capital, Tenochtitlán, the
Aztecs built spectacular palaces. They also built
temples to the gods all over the empire. The
Aztecs believed that sacrificing humans, usually
prisoners caught in battle, kept the gods happy.

Where is the lost city of the Incas?

The lost city of the Incas—Machu Picchu—lies high in the Andes Mountains in South America. The ancient Incas ruled a mighty empire between 1430 and 1530. After the collapse of the empire, the location of the city was lost to the rest of the world. It was only rediscovered in 1911 by the American explorer Hiram Bingham.

DID YOU KNOW?
Aztec emperors drank hot chocolate, but it was made from ground-up cocoa beans, honey, and chili, so it was a lot spicier than hot chocolate today!

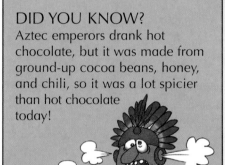

What happened to the Aztecs and Incas?

The Aztecs and Incas lost their power in the 1500s when Spanish soldiers arrived in ships. The Spanish set out to conquer them and steal their gold. Within a few years, the Spanish had destroyed most of the Aztec and Inca buildings, stolen their treasure, and taken over their empires.

RIGHT Inca warriors were no match for Spanish soldiers armed with rifles and on horseback.

CHINESE RULERS

BELOW The terra-cotta soldiers are a life-size model army built for the tomb of the first emperor, Shihuangdi.

Who ruled China in the past?

From 221 BC until AD 1912, China was ruled by a series of emperors. These men were powerful and were called sons of heaven. During this time, China was one of the largest, richest, and most advanced civilizations in the world. The Chinese people believed their country was the center of the world and they thought that all foreigners were barbarians.

Where was the Silk Route?

The Silk Route was a series of tracks that ran westward from China, over mountains and deserts, to ports in the Middle East and around the Mediterranean Sea. Chinese merchants transported silk, porcelain (fine pottery), and other goods along the Silk Route to sell elsewhere. They brought goods, such as gold, jade, and horses, back to China.

KEY
— Silk Route

EUROPE
Constantinople
Rome
MEDITERRANEAN SEA
Antioch
Palmyra
Tyre
Alexandria
MIDDLE EAST
AFRICA
Bukhara
Kashgar
Merv
Leh
Khotan
Miran
Turfan
Hami
Dunhuang
Chang'an
CHINA
INDIA
ARABIAN SEA
INDIAN OCEAN

ABOVE Trade along the Silk Route began in about 100 BC and continued to flourish until the 1400s.

What did the Chinese invent?

The Chinese were great inventors and made many important discoveries. They invented canals to transport goods around the country. They invented gunpowder, flamethrowers, and exploding bombs to defend themselves. The Chinese developed paper-making and paper currency, and made a seismograph to sense when an earthquake might happen. They also created silk, fireworks, and the game of soccer!

LEFT Chinese paper was made from plants such as bamboo.

Why was the Great Wall built?

The Great Wall of China was built to keep out invaders from the north. It began as a series of separate walls that were joined up in around 220 BC. Along the wall, there were many watch towers. If a guard saw danger, he would light a fire to signal the next tower. This tower would light a fire, too, and so on, until everyone was alerted.

DID YOU KNOW?
The Chinese invented pasta, too. Explorer Marco Polo brought the recipe for noodles back to Europe from China after visiting there in the 1200s.

THE SPREAD OF ISLAM

When was Islam founded?

Islam was founded by the prophet Muhammad in the Middle East in the AD 600s. Within 400 years, the Islamic religion had spread far and wide. The Islamic rulers, called caliphs, led great armies that conquered a region stretching from central Asia, across North Africa, and into Spain. The followers of Islam believe in one God, Allah, and are known as Muslims.

BELOW This map shows how far Islam had spread by about AD 1000.

EUROPE
SPAIN
Córdoba
Carthage
SYRIA
Alexandria
Jerusalem
Baghdad
PERSIA
EGYPT
AFRICA
Makkah
OMAN
ARABIAN SEA
YEMEN

BELOW The Great Mosque in Makkah can hold up to 1 million worshippers at a time.

DID YOU KNOW?
In a palace in Baghdad, there was a huge tree made of gold and silver, filled with mechanical golden birds. The birds chirped to cheer up the caliph if he felt sad.

Which is Islam's most important city?

Makkah, in modern-day Saudi Arabia, is Islam's most holy city. It is where the prophet Muhammad was born in AD 570. Every year, millions of Muslims travel to Makkah on a sacred journey called a *hajj*, or pilgrimage. Muslims are expected to visit Makkah at least once in their lives, if possible.

What was Muslim art like?

Pictures of people and animals were forbidden by Islam, so Muslim art had its own style. Buildings, pottery, and carpets were decorated with patterns of flowers and leaves, geometric designs, or beautiful writing. This elaborate writing, known as calligraphy, was usually a quote from the Qur'an. Books were often highly decorated in the same style.

ABOVE Carved patterns and calligraphy decorate the walls at the Alhambra Palace in Spain.

Where do Muslims worship?

BELOW The Dome of the Rock in Jerusalem is a sacred place for Muslims. The mosque's dome is covered in gold.

Muslims worship in a sacred building called a mosque. At a mosque, Muslims pray and learn about the Islamic holy book, the Qur'an. As Islam spread around the world, many different styles of mosques were built, but most have a courtyard surrounded by four halls. Many mosques have towers called minarets, from which criers call the faithful to prayer.

141

THE MIDDLE AGES

When were the Middle Ages?

The Middle Ages were a long period of history between about AD 410 and 1500 which divides ancient and modern times. The period lasted from the end of the Roman Empire until the start of the Renaissance, when people started to take an interest in the cultures of the ancient world.

What was life like in medieval Europe?

Medieval life was organized by the "feudal system." The Church and the kings were at the top of this system and owned most of the land. Next in importance were the nobles, who fought for the kings and in return were given land and castles. At the bottom were the peasants, who worked the land for the nobles.

ABOVE In the Middle Ages, many large and ornate buildings, such as this cathedral, were built in a style known as Gothic.

How did knights protect castles?

Knights were soldiers who belonged to private armies owned by the nobles and kings who lived in the castles. The knights rode horses and wore suits of metal armor for protection. When a castle was attacked, the knights were the last line of defense. First, the attackers had to get across the moat (water-filled ditch) and over the high walls.

DID YOU KNOW?
Legends about outlaws, such as Robin Hood, became popular at this time because poor people's lives were so bad and many of the rich lords were very unpopular.

What were the Crusades?

The Crusades were a series of wars between Muslims and Christians over the Muslim-controlled land around the holy city of Jerusalem in the Middle East. In 1095, the leader of the Catholic Church, Pope Urban II, ordered Christian armies from Europe to capture Jerusalem and the Holy Land from the Muslims. After some success, the Christians finally lost the land to the Muslims in the 1200s.

LEFT The Muslim leader Saladin led an army that captured Jerusalem from the Christians in 1187.

AFRICAN KINGDOMS

The ruins of Great Zimbabwe can still be seen today.

What was Africa's greatest kingdom?

The rulers of the Shona kingdom in southeast Africa ruled a great empire between AD 1200 and 1600. Shona kings built the great fortress city of Great Zimbabwe, which was surrounded by walls 65 feet high. The city's inhabitants mined gold nearby and farmed the surrounding lands. Great Zimbabwe was also an important religious center.

RIGHT A dhow was the kind of ship used to trade at the time. They are still used today.

How did African cities become rich?

African cities traded ivory, gold, salt, and slaves with Arab traders to the east. Goods were carried by boat down the major rivers or in long camel trains across the desert. Some of these cities became so powerful that they controlled large areas of land around them.

What are the Benin Bronzes?

The Benin Bronzes are statues or masks made of brass and bronze. They come from the area that is now Nigeria in West Africa, where they were used to decorate the king's magnificent palace and family altars. The Kingdom of Benin was powerful from 1400 to 1900, when it traded pepper, ivory, and leopard skins with Europe. Many of the bronzes depict scenes of court life, showing kings with their wives, servants, and soldiers.

Where can you see churches cut from rock?

You can still see churches carved out of solid rock in Ethiopia, East Africa. The people of Ethiopia had been Christians since the AD 300s. The 11 churches carved out of solid rock in the ancient city of Labilela took 24 years to complete. Some are below ground and are connected by a network of tunnels and passageways.

ABOVE Thousands of pilgrims still visit the rock churches of Ethiopia today.

INDIAN EMPERORS

What was the Mughal Empire?

The Mughal Empire covered most of India from 1526 until 1857. The Mughals were originally from Mongolia and they followed the Muslim religion, whereas most people in India at the time were Hindus. The most successful Mughal emperor was Akbar, who took the throne when he was only 13. He conquered many new lands and made India very rich.

RIGHT The Mughals built many magnificent palaces. "Mughal" is the North Indian word for "Mongol," a person who comes from Mongolia.

Who was the first emperor?

The first Mughal emperor was Babur, who was related to the famous Genghis Khan. Babur invaded India in the early 1500s. He was vicious in battle but was a good ruler. He wrote poetry and wanted to lead a peaceful empire. Babur allowed new Hindu temples to be built and banned the killing of cows because they are sacred to Hindus.

BELOW The Taj Mahal is in Agra in northern India. It took 22,000 workers more than 20 years to build it.

When was the Taj Mahal built?

The white marble Taj Mahal was built between 1630 and 1653 by the fifth Mughal emperor, Shah Jahan. He built it as a tomb for his beloved wife, who died giving birth to their fifteenth child. The Mughal emperors used their wealth to build many splendid forts, mosques, and tombs in India, using craftsmen from all over their empire.

DID YOU KNOW?
It is said that 1,000 elephants were used to deliver all the marble, jade, crystal, turquoise, diamonds, and other stones and gems used to build the Taj Mahal!

BELOW A map of the Mughal Empire during the reign of Aurangzeb.

How large was the Mughal Empire?

During the reign of Aurangzeb, between 1658 and 1707, the Mughal Empire reached its peak in terms of size, covering most of modern-day India. After that, the empire started to break up because of wars and invasions. By the end of the 1700s, the Mughals ruled a small region around Delhi. The last Mughal emperor was Bahadur Shah II, who ruled from 1837 until he was exiled by the British in 1857.

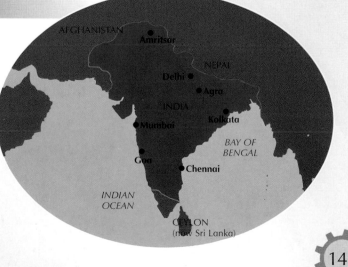

AFGHANISTAN
Amritsar
NEPAL
Delhi
Agra
INDIA
Kolkata
Mumbai
BAY OF BENGAL
Goa
Chennai
INDIAN OCEAN
CEYLON (now Sri Lanka)

AGE OF EXPLORATION

BELOW Early explorers traveled west to North and South America and south to travel around Africa and into the Indian Ocean.

What was the Age of Exploration?

The Age of Exploration was a time from the 1500s until the 1700s, when people from Europe began to explore the rest of the world. They sailed in huge ships called galleons in search of rare goods, such as spices and sources of silver and gold. Some explorers set out to make maps of the world and others went in order to spread their religious beliefs.

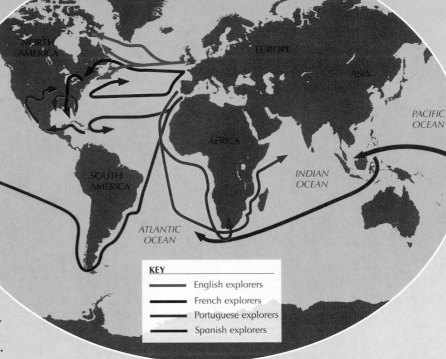

NORTH AMERICA
EUROPE
ASIA
PACIFIC OCEAN
AFRICA
SOUTH AMERICA
INDIAN OCEAN
ATLANTIC OCEAN

KEY
—— English explorers
—— French explorers
—— Portuguese explorers
—— Spanish explorers

LEFT Blackbeard was one of the most famous pirates. He put matches in his beard to scare his enemies during battle.

DID YOU KNOW?
In the 1400s, people thought the world was flat. They believed that ships would sail off the edge if they went too far!

Who were the real pirates of the Caribbean?

The real pirates of the Caribbean were robbers who stole from ships at sea. They fired at and boarded galleons carrying valuable goods back to Europe and stole their cargo. They made the sailors "walk the plank," forcing them to walk off a board into the sea and to certain death.

ABOVE The high castle at the back of a galleon housed the living quarters for the captain and officers.

What were galleons like?

Galleons were huge ships with castles, or towers, at the front and back. A galleon had three or four tall masts and several decks. One deck held the guns and cannons. The ordinary sailors slept on hammocks in cramped lower decks and the ships were dirty and crawling with mice.

What did explorers eat?

Explorers mainly ate food that had been preserved by drying, salting, smoking, or pickling because fresh food would not keep on long journeys. The lack of fresh fruit and vegetables meant that many sailors got scurvy, a disease that made their teeth fall out and gave them a lot of sores.

BELOW The British navy gave its sailors oranges and limes to eat to prevent scurvy. Because of this, the British were nicknamed "limeys."

DISCOVERING AMERICA

ABOVE Christopher Columbus captained the *Santa Maria*, one of three ships in his fleet.

When was America discovered by Europeans?

The first Europeans in the Americas were probably the Vikings, who settled on the northwest coast of North America in the AD 1000s. However, more famous is the arrival of Italian explorer Christopher Columbus in 1492. He was seeking a new route from Europe to Asia when his ships landed on an island in the Caribbean Sea. Columbus believed he was in the East Indies, near Japan or China, and so called the islanders Indians.

Who were the Pilgrim Fathers?

The Pilgrim Fathers were a group of people from England who sailed to North America in 1620. They were looking for a place to live where they would be free to follow their religion and where they could live by their own laws. Many of the settlers died in the first winter. The following year, survivors celebrated their first harvest, called Thanksgiving, with native people from a local tribe.

BELOW The Pilgrim Fathers built simple homes of wood, similar to the ones in this modern-day reconstruction.

DID YOU KNOW?
The Statue of Liberty was given to the United States by France on the 100th anniversary of the Declaration of Independence.

ABOVE The Declaration of Independence was a document signed by American leaders on July 4, 1776.

What are the United States of America?

The United States of America, or the USA, is made up of 50 states, or regions. The term "USA" was first used in the Declaration of Independence in 1776, when the American people first declared their freedom from British rule. The Americans went to war with the British and finally won their independence and the right to govern themselves.

Why was there a Civil War?

One of the main reasons for the Civil War of 1861–65 was slavery. At this time, all people in the northern states were free, but in the South, black people still worked as slaves. When the South tried to form a separate nation, the North went to war to keep the United States together. In 1863, the North announced that it would free the slaves when it won the war.

INDUSTRIAL REVOLUTION

What was the Industrial Revolution?

The Industrial Revolution was the time when machines were increasingly used to do work that had been done by people. The change began in Britain in the late 1700s and eventually spread throughout the world. The new machinery included large steam-powered looms for making cotton fabric quickly and cheaply.

RIGHT The invention of the steam engine created a way to power the new machines.

When were the first factories built?

The first factories were built around 1770 to house the big new machines of the Industrial Revolution. In the factories, large numbers of workers could be gathered together to operate the machines. Many poor people moved from the country to work in the factories, living in dirty, cramped homes in the overcrowded cities.

How did railroads make a difference?

Railroads were important to the Industrial Revolution because they transported coal and raw materials to the factories, and carried finished goods away again to sell. The trains allowed people to move around the country to find work. The first steam locomotive built in the USA in 1830 was called the *Best Friend of Charleston*. By 1869, tracks ran across country from coast to coast.

DID YOU KNOW?
Before railroads, canals were built to carry coal from mines to factories and towns. Between 1760 and 1840, almost 4,350 miles of canals were built in Britain.

Where did children work?

Many children worked in factories and coal mines in Britain in the 1800s. Some children as young as five years old worked up to 16 hours a day. They were often treated badly by their bosses and many were injured by the machines. In 1833, the British government passed a law to prevent children under nine from working in factories.

RIGHT Children were used in mines to drag carts full of coal along cramped tunnels.

MODERN TIMES

Over 8 million soldiers died in enemy gunfire on both sides in World War I in 1914–18. This huge number was so horrific that people believed that it was the war to end all wars. But the world went to war again in 1939–45. World War II ended after the USA dropped the world's first atomic bomb on the Japanese city of Hiroshima, killing about 140,000 people.

What was the Cold War?

The Cold War was a period of great tension after World War II between the United States and Russia (then called the Soviet Union). These two powerful nations had different political beliefs, and each feared that the other would try to force their way of life on them. Although the Soviet Union and the USA did not actually fight, many were worried that the tension might develop into war.

BELOW The Berlin Wall divided the German city into Soviet and non-Soviet sections. It was pulled down in 1989, when the Cold War ended.

How has the political world changed?

The last 100 years have seen great changes in the political shape of the world. Many countries that were once governed by European nations became independent. In other countries, regimes that oppressed certain groups of people were overthrown, such as the apartheid system in South Africa.

ABOVE The apartheid system denied black South Africans their human rights. In 1990, the lead campaigner against apartheid, Nelson Mandela, was released from prison, signaling the end of the oppressive system.

DID YOU KNOW?
A time traveler from 1900 would be amazed by inventions that have appeared since then, such as computers, cell phones, televisions, and aircraft.

Why is the world shrinking?

Some people describe the modern world as shrinking because improvements in transportation and communication make it feel smaller. Telephones and computers carry information worldwide in an instant. Advances in transportation mean that people can travel thousands of miles on planes, cars, and trains quicker than ever before.

PEOPLE AND PLACES

Our planet is incredibly varied. Not just among the animals and the different habitats of the world, but among people and the places people live. This variety is what makes our world a rich and fascinating place. Between one country and another you will find that people eat different foods, enjoy different styles of music, dress in their own unique ways, and believe in different things. But in some ways people everywhere are very similar, because they all try to lead happy lives.

AROUND THE WORLD

How many people are there in the world?

There are more than 6.5 billion people in the world! Many people today have more food and better health care than they had in the past and so they live longer than before. As more people live longer, the number of children being born is higher than the number of people who die. This means that the planet's population is increasing.

DID YOU KNOW?
The smallest country in the world is the Vatican City in Rome, Italy. It only covers a total area of about 100 acres—about the size of 50 football fields.

BELOW The spectacular cathedral of St. Basil is in Moscow, capital of Russia, the world's largest country.

Which are the world's largest countries?

The world's largest countries by area are Russia, Canada, the United States, and China. The largest is Russia—it is almost twice the size of Canada. Russia has a variety of landscapes, from vast plains to mountain ranges. Russia's Lake Baikal, the world's deepest lake, contains one-fifth of the Earth's fresh water.

Where is the largest population?

The country with the largest population in the world is China. Over 1.3 billion people live here. Most are Chinese but there are 55 different ethnic groups altogether. Since the 1970s, China has tried to slow down its population growth by encouraging couples to have just one child. By 2030 India, which has over a billion people, will probably have a larger population than China.

LEFT Chinese cities, such as Shanghai, are among the world's wealthiest and fastest-growing cities.

How do new countries form?

Sometimes a new country forms when two or more separate countries join together. Some new countries form when an area becomes independent of a larger country and starts to rule itself. This happened in the 1990s when Yugoslavia began splitting into separate countries (left). In the past, some countries conquered other lands and ruled over them as part of an empire. When the empires collapsed these lands became new independent countries.

159

WHERE PEOPLE LIVE

KEY

MORE THAN 1,300

650-1,300

260-650

130-260

65-130

5-65

LESS THAN 5

0

LEFT This map shows how many people live per square mile around the world.

Is the world's population spread evenly?

No. Most parts of the world are empty of people, while others, such as Tokyo, in Japan, are very overcrowded. Today most people in North America, Europe, and Australia live in towns and cities. In other parts of the world the majority of people live in the countryside. Cities are constantly growing as people move into them to find work.

Did some people live up mountains?

People live in the mountains in many parts of the world. They have to travel over steep roads to get anywhere and cope with harsh weather in winter. Humans have found ways of living in all kinds of places. They learned to farm steep land by building terraces (left).

160

ABOVE This village in Cambodia is built on stilts above a river.

Are homes different around the world?

Yes! Some house styles look similar, but in many places houses have to be built to suit the weather, the land, or the number of people. People who live in places that sometimes flood build their houses on stilts, or wooden legs, to raise them above the water. On mountains, people build houses with sloping roofs so the snow will slide off.

What is a nomad?

A nomad is a person who does not settle in one place. In parts of Asia, some nomads travel around in search of fresh places for their animals to graze. In Africa, they may travel to find new water sources. In European countries, some groups of Roma (gypsies) and other traveling people live in caravans or mobile homes and travel from place to place.

RIGHT A yurt is a type of portable home used by the nomad people of Mongolia.

DID YOU KNOW?
A megacity is a city with more than 10 million inhabitants. Today, there are about 20 megacities around the world.

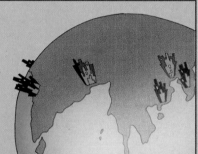

161

GOVERNMENTS

Where are governments based?

Governments are based in their country's capital city. Government representatives from the rest of the country meet together in offices in the capital to make decisions and discuss matters, such as new laws. Because the capital city is an important place, other business and financial institutions set up there, too. Many capital cities become extremely large. Mexico City, for example, is home to about 20 million people.

ABOVE The Capitol Building in Washington, D.C., is home to the United States government.

Why do people vote?

People vote in elections to choose people to lead them, for example, in a government. In what is called a democracy, voters have a choice of leaders. When chosen, the leaders work for the people. The opposite of a democracy is a dictatorship. Dictatorships do not allow people to choose their leader and one person may control the whole country.

RIGHT Governments make decisions after a debate like this one, in the House of Commons, United Kingdom.

DID YOU KNOW?
The first country in the world to give women the right to vote in national elections was New Zealand, in 1893, followed by Australia, in 1902.

What do governments do?

Governments run countries. They make laws and defend their country using armed forces. They are responsible for public services, such as schools and hospitals. Governments raise money to do these things by charging people taxes. A government is usually led by a president or prime minister.

Do kings and queens still rule countries?

There are still a small number of countries in the world, such as Saudi Arabia, that are personally ruled by a king. Today, most of the world's remaining kingdoms are democracies where the king or queen is the head of the country, but daily government is carried out by people elected by voters. There are at least 50 kings and queens in the world. They inherit their title when a previous king or queen dies or retires.

LEFT King Carl Gustav and Queen Silvia are the king and queen of Sweden, a country ruled by a democratic government.

THE WORLD OF WORK

ABOVE A giant combine harvester cuts the wheat fields on the vast plains of the American Midwest.

Where are the biggest farms?

The biggest farms in the world are in the United States and Canada. In the United States, for example, farmers grow immense fields of crops, such as wheat. To grow such large amounts of food, these farms rely on modern machines and chemical sprays that get rid of weeds and insect pests. This type of farming is called intensive farming.

What is the world's biggest fishing net?

Some giant fishing boats have nets that stretch as wide as a football field! These are dragged through the ocean to scoop up fish. Fishing is an important industry for many people around the world. There are about 3 million people working in fishing boats in the sea. They catch so many fish that in some parts of the oceans fish have become scarce.

164

Where is the world's busiest factory?

Many people say that China is like the world's busiest and biggest factory. A factory is a place that makes many copies of the same thing to sell. Vast amounts of the goods the world buys come from China, including clothing, watches, and cell phones. Over half of the world's cameras and a third of the world's televisions are made in China.

LEFT The Eiffel Tower in Paris, France, brings in much money from tourism.

Is tourism important?

Tourism is an important industry all over the world because it creates many jobs, for example, in hotels and restaurants. It also brings in money from foreign visitors. The most visited destination in the world for foreign tourists is Paris, in France. People come here to enjoy the famous museums, palaces, and the Eiffel Tower.

DID YOU KNOW?
Some cattle and sheep farms in Australia are so big farmers use planes instead of tractors to check on their animals.

RICH AND POOR

Why are some countries richer than others?

There are many reasons why some countries are richer than others. One reason is that they have "natural resources." These can be valuable things, such as oil, coal, trees, or diamonds. People can dig up or harvest these resources and sell them, or make them into goods they can sell. But it is important to remember that even in rich countries there are still poor people.

RIGHT This oil refinery produces valuable barrels of oil that a country can sell.

Why people are hungry?

Experts estimate that 850 million people across the world do not have enough to eat. Some people go hungry because they live in countries where it is very dry and difficult to grow food. Sometimes people go hungry because there is a war in their country and supplies of food are cut off. Most people who are underfed are poor and live in less-developed countries.

DID YOU KNOW?
There should be enough food in the world to feed everyone, but some people are not getting enough. Other people are eating too much and becoming sick because they are too fat.

What are shanty towns?

Shanty towns are groups of homes built from scrap materials, such as pieces of wood and sheets of metal or plastic. They are often found on the edge of cities. Shanty towns are made by people who came to find work but who remain poor. These towns often have no running water. Fires sometimes break out because most people here use fire for cooking and warmth.

Who helps people in need?

Groups of people working for charities raise money to help people in need. Most try to provide the means for people to rebuild their own lives. For example, they might give farmers tools or seeds, or provide training for someone to learn a new skill. They also help educate children in less-developed countries so they can get a job when they grow up.

GETTING AROUND

What is the fastest train?

The Maglev train in Shanghai, China, is the fastest train in the world. Maglev is short for magnetic levitation. This train floats just above a magnetic rail. It can go at speeds of up to 268 miles per hour. Many trains are used by commuters—people who travel into cities to work every day. In Japan's capital city, Tokyo, 9 out of 10 workers travel to and from their offices by train.

BELOW So many people in American cities own cars that long traffic jams develop every day.

How many vehicles are there in the world?

There are about 1 billion motor vehicles being driven on the roads today. Cars, buses, and other vehicles, such as planes, release exhaust fumes that cause air pollution. These fumes are upsetting the balance of gases in the atmosphere and are causing global warming.

TRUCKS
USE
RIGHT
LANES

SPEED
LIMIT
50

Which is the world's busiest airport?

Atlanta, in the United States, is the world's busiest airport because it has the highest number of passengers passing through its doors—more than 88 million people a year. More people travel by plane today than ever before. The fastest passenger plane ever in service was the Concorde, which could fly from London to New York in just over three hours!

DID YOU KNOW?
In Beijing, China, residents own more than 8 million bicycles. Worldwide there are more than a billion bicycles in use today!

ABOVE Jet aircraft are a major cause of air pollution.

Which is the most common form of transportation?

Cycling is the most common form of transportation in the world. Bicycles are widely used in countries where people cannot afford a car. Bicycles can tow loads and travel over places with no roads. Many people choose to ride bicycles to keep in shape or to reduce the pollution caused by vehicle traffic.

KEEPING IN TOUCH

How do we communicate?

Communication happens when we pass signals to each other. It is something we do every day. We communicate through speech and through written words, through hand gestures, and with the expressions on our faces. People with limited hearing use a special form of communication by making hand signs. They can also read the shape of our lips when we speak.

How many different languages are there?

There may be as many as 8,000 in the world. In many countries, people may speak the national language and also a local dialect (form of speech). The most common language in the world is Chinese (Mandarin). Outside China the most widely spoken language is English.

RIGHT Some of these signs in Ireland are written in English and also in the old language of Ireland, Gaelic.

...them right to left?

People who read books in Arabic or Hebrew read from right to left. Some languages, such as Japanese, are written from the top of the page to the bottom. Different languages often have different alphabets. The English alphabet has 26 letters but the alphabet used in Cambodia has 74!

LEFT Many people in China and Japan practice calligraphy—the art of writing words beautifully.

...phone calls travel across the world?

Communications satellites in space pick up telephone signals and transfer them to receivers on the other side of the world. Today we can communicate instantly with people far away. The satellites are also used for Internet connections so that people all over the world can keep in touch using e-mail.

DID YOU KNOW?
Esperanto is a special language that does not belong to one country but was invented over 100 years ago as an international language.

Satellite

Receiver

RELIGIONS OF THE WORLD

Where do Christians worship?

Christians usually worship in a church. They praise God in prayer and music, and listen to readings from the Bible. There are also holy ceremonies, such as the Eucharist, in which a priest offers people wine and bread in memory of the last supper Jesus Christ shared with his followers.

ABOVE This is the Church of the Holy Sepulcher in Jerusalem. The city is considered holy by Christians, Muslims, and Jews.

BELOW The Wailing Wall in Jerusalem is the holiest place for Jews. It is all that remains of an ancient Jewish temple.

What is a synagogue?

A synagogue is a building where followers of the Jewish religion gather to worship. Jews believe that there is a single God who created the universe. On Saturdays, Jewish people go to their synagogue to take part in a service. Jewish religious leaders are called rabbis. They lead the prayers and read from the Torah, the Jewish holy book.

172

How many times a day do Muslims pray?

Muslims try to pray five times a day. They are the followers of the religion called Islam. Muslims can pray anywhere, but it is especially good to pray with other people in a mosque—the Muslim place of worship. Muslims believe that there is only one God, called Allah. Their laws are based on the teachings of their holy book, the Qur'an.

RIGHT A Muslim at prayer.

Who are Hindu holy men?

Hindu holy men, known as saddhus, devote their lives to the Hindu religion. These men own nothing. They wander from place to place and are given food by other Hindus. Hindu people worship images of their gods in temples. At home, many also have a shrine where they can make offerings of food or flowers to their gods.

BELOW Hindu holy men in India pray before a shrine.

DID YOU KNOW?
Followers of Buddhism have made statues of their teacher, the Buddha, all over the world. Some are three times higher than the Statue of Liberty in the United States!

FESTIVALS AND SPECIAL DAYS

What happens at Passover?

Passover is an important religious festival that Jews celebrate with special prayers and food. It begins with the Seder—a meal and a story about the history of Passover. Passover is the time the Jews were led out of slavery in Egypt by the prophet Moses. The festival lasts for eight days.

When is Chinese New Year?

Chinese New Year is in February. Before the New Year celebrations begin, people clean their homes to chase away evil spirits. During the celebrations, people share special meals, give each other gifts, and set off fireworks. There are also dances with large dragon and lion costumes. The dragon, a symbol of strength, is thought to repel evil and bring good luck.

RIGHT These girls are decorating Easter eggs with colored paints.

Why do we eat chocolate eggs at Easter?

People eat chocolate eggs at Easter because eggs represent new life. Easter Sunday commemorates the day Jesus Christ came to life again, after he was crucified (nailed to a cross). Easter is the most important festival in the Christian calendar. In churches, Christians celebrate by singing special hymns.

DID YOU KNOW?
Although Myanmar (Burma) in South Asia is usually dry and hot in April, it is always wet at the New Year celebrations, called Thingyan, because people spray each other with water!

What is the festival of light?

The festival of light, called Diwali, celebrates the coming of the Hindu New Year in October or November. Diwali lasts over five days. Stories told during this time celebrate the victory of good over evil and knowledge over ignorance. People decorate buildings with candles and colored lights, and they make delicious treats.

ART AND MUSIC

Do dances tell stories?

Yes, many dances in different cultures across the world are used to tell stories. In India, kathakali dances tell stories of gods and demons. And some ballets, such as *The Nutcracker*, use graceful movements to tell a fairy tale. Other types of dances are used to express a mood or a feeling or are just for fun. Certain dances are only performed at celebrations, such as weddings.

RIGHT Kathakali dancing is a spectacular combination of drama, dance, music, and ritual.

What is street theater?

Street theater is when people perform plays in outdoor public places, such as shopping centers. In a real theater there are lights and plenty of space for props and costumes. In street theater actors have very simple props and often have to shout to be heard. People buy a ticket to go into a theater, but usually pay street performers what they think a show is worth after it is over.

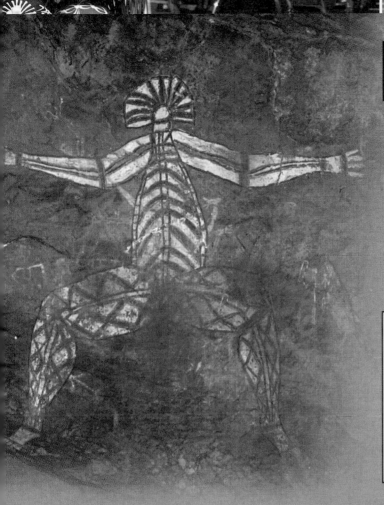

Where do dreamtime paintings come from?

Dreamtime paintings are made by the Aboriginal peoples of Australia. These artists use many dots to form symbols and shapes that describe a time in the past before there were people, when spirit gods created the rivers, rocks, and mountains. Like many types of painting, these images are powerful because they tell stories without using words.

DID YOU KNOW?
The oldest musical instrument of all is the human voice! People have always sung songs. Sometimes people sing together in choirs of hundreds of singers.

LEFT Steel drum music began in Trinidad and Tobago in the 1940s. It is influenced by African drum music.

What is "world music"?

"World music" is music that has an international appeal but is the traditional sound of one particular country. Sometimes the traditional music of a country is connected to a certain instrument. In Indonesia, for example, gamelan musicians play music on bronze xylophones. In Spain, flamenco is played on guitars and dancers accompany the music. In Jamica, steel drum bands make a rich sound.

177

CHILDREN AROUND THE WORLD

What games do children play?

Around the world, children play a great variety of games. Some, such as marbles, soccer, and other ball games, are played in nearly every country. In some countries, children play with expensive toys or computer games. In other countries, such as South Africa, some children make their own toys from recycled pieces of wire and cans.

RIGHT This American boy is practicing his baseball pitch. Baseball is a national sport in the United States.

Why do some children work?

Some children work to help their parents. They may help with farm chores before they go to school. Some children work all day instead of going to school. This is often because their parents are poor and need help to earn money. In many countries, this is illegal and young people may only work part-time.

178

When do children start school?

The age at which children start elementary school varies between countries. In India, children start school at the age of five. In Norway and Russia, children start at seven. In elementary school, children learn to read and write, although for some children this may be in a different language from the one they speak at home.

BELOW In an elementary school, children may learn all their subjects from a single teacher.

DID YOU KNOW?
The legal age at which a child becomes an adult varies between countries. In Iran it is 15, in the United States and most of Europe it is 18, while in some parts of Africa it is 13!

BELOW Pupils learn from the blackboard in this outside class in Africa.

Where do children learn outside?

In some of the world's poorer countries, classes take place outside because there are few school buildings. In parts of Nepal, some people live in remote areas, and children walk several miles to school and back each day. Some schools may have fewer classes because they may be short of books, tables, pens, and pencils.

179

CLOTHES THAT PEOPLE WEAR

What is national dress?

National dress is the clothing traditionally worn by people in a particular country. Around the world today many people wear similar sorts of clothes, but some people still wear traditional dress every day or on special occasions, such as festivals, weddings, or religious celebrations. Traditional dress does not change with fashion.

LEFT This Japanese girl is wearing a traditional kimono (gown) tied with an obi (sash).

Who wears saris?

In many hot countries, people wear long loose clothes to keep out the heat of the sun. These clothes are sometimes white or light-colored because light colors reflect instead of absorb heat, and this helps to keep people cool. It is also important to choose natural fabrics, such as cotton or linen, because these fabrics are cool and better at absorbing perspiration.

When do people wear uniforms?

Across the world many people wear uniforms when they are at work or school. Uniforms are important for police officers, for example, so we can find them if we need help. Some uniforms are designed to be practical. For example, firefighters' uniforms protect them from heat. Many schools have uniforms so that rich and poor are dressed alike.

LEFT These firefighters wear distinctive orange uniforms that also protect them.

DID YOU KNOW?
On a cold day, about 70 percent of your total body heat is lost through your head. That is why it is important to wear a hat in the winter.

RIGHT This Sikh woman is wearing a traditional red wedding dress.

Why are some colors special?

The color of a piece of clothing can be special when it is worn for particular ceremonies or reasons. For example, black is the traditional color of mourning and is worn as a mark of respect at funerals in western countries. In China and India, people wear white for funerals and in parts of Africa they wear red. And while white is the traditional color for wedding dresses in western countries, in China it is red.

THE FOOD WE EAT

What are staple foods?

Staple foods are filling foods that provide energy. They are usually carbohydrates, such as rice. The staples people eat are those that grow well in their local area. Corn is a staple in Central America and potatoes are staples in North America and Europe.

Where do pineapples grow?

Pineapples and other tropical fruit, such as bananas and mangoes, grow best in countries where it is warm all year. Different crops need different climates and soils. That is why some foods are more common in some places than others. For example, apples grow better in temperate, or milder, climates.

DID YOU KNOW?
About half the world's people eat insects as part of their diet. In total, about 1,500 different species of insect are eaten by people in various parts of the world.

LEFT These farmers carry pineapples on a special rack that does not bruise the fruit.

182

Who doesn't eat meat?

Vegetarians are people who do not eat meat. People of certain religions also have rules about what foods they eat. Hindus do not eat beef because for them the cow is a holy animal (left). Muslims and Jews do not eat pork because it is considered an unclean animal. Traditionally, Catholics do not eat red meat on Friday and this is why fish is a popular dinner at the end of the week.

Who eats with chopsticks?

People in East Asian countries, such as China, eat with chopsticks—as do people in many other parts of the world when they eat East Asian food. Chopsticks are held between the thumb and index finger. In the West, most people eat with knives, forks, and spoons. In India, many people eat with their fingers.

BELOW Picking up slippery noodles with chopsticks takes some practice!

183

COUNTRY CONNECTIONS

How are countries connected?

One of the ways in which countries are connected is through trade. For example, bananas only grow in tropical regions. People in Europe and North America like to eat bananas and depend upon the banana farmers to grow the fruit. The farmers rely upon the countries that buy the fruit because this trade pays their wages. This is called being interdependent.

How does international trade work?

International trade is what happens when a company sells goods to consumers in another country. These goods are called exports. When a country imports goods, it means they buy them from another country. Factories and farms produce goods to sell across the world. Their goods are transported in huge container ships and airplanes.

BELOW Large cranes are used to unload the goods from this container ship.

184

What is fair trade?

Fair trade is when the people who grow or make products for export get paid a fair price. Fair trade companies make sure that workers are treated fairly and are not made to work in dangerous conditions or for long hours. Many fair trade products have special labels so that shoppers can choose to support these standards of fairness.

RIGHT An East Asian fair trade farmer harvests a rice crop.

DID YOU KNOW?
Many of us eat food that that has traveled between 1,500 and 2,500 miles from the farm where it was grown!

Are people the same across the world?

People everywhere are connected because we all share the same basic needs. People who live in the same country may be defined by their nationality, such as Indian or Chinese, but today many different peoples live in one country and many countries are "multicultural."

185

SCIENCE AND TECHNOLOGY

The world around us behaves according to scientific laws. Scientists have discovered many of these laws, and are making new discoveries all the time. We develop technology using our understanding of science and the forces, such as magnetism, gravity, and electricity, which shape our lives. Whenever you turn on a light, log onto the Internet, or speak to your friends on a cell phone, it has all been made possible by science.

THE WORLD AROUND US

What are things made of?

Everything, from water or air to a whale or a cell phone, is made of tiny particles called atoms. There are over 100 different kinds of atoms, which are in turn made of smaller parts called subatomic particles. Two or more atoms join together to make a molecule. The things around us are solids, liquids, or gases, depending on the arrangement of the atoms and molecules inside them.

Buildings need to be made from hard solids, such as stone.

BELOW An atom is made of subatomic particles. Particles called electrons circle around the center, called the nucleus.

Nucleus

Electron

Why are stones hard?

Stones are hard because they are solids. Atoms or molecules in solids are packed tightly and neatly together. This means solids hold their own shape. Some solids are bendable or squishy, such as rubber or feathers. The hardness of a solid depends on how tightly their atoms are held together.

honey runny?

Honey is runny because it is a liquid. The molecules inside a liquid are less tightly packed than they are in a solid, and are not rigidly linked. That is why liquids can flow and take the shape of the container we pour them into. Some liquids are thick, such as honey. Others are thin, such as water.

DID YOU KNOW?
Atoms are so tiny that, even if you put four million atoms side-by-side, they would only be the width of a pinhead!

OW do loons float?

Helium balloons float because the gas inside them is lighter than air. In all gases, molecules move around quickly in all directions. Gases do not stay in one shape as solids do. They can spread out to fill any shape or space. In a hot-air balloon, the air molecules spread out as they heat up. As there are fewer molecules inside the balloon than outside, it floats.

LEFT Hot-air balloons float because the hot air inside them is lighter than the cold air around them.

189

FORCES AND MOVEMENT

When do things move?

Things only move when a force is applied to them. Forces are pushes or pulls in a particular direction. A flag blows when the wind pushes it. A door opens when you pull it. Animals move when their feet push against the ground, their wings push against air, or their fins push against the water around them.

How do forces work?

Forces work in pairs. They push or pull in opposite directions. When pairs of forces are equal they are said to be balanced. Tug-of-war teams remain still when each pulls with the same strength. A team falls when one side is stronger and the forces are unbalanced. Forces are also balanced when things move at one speed in the same direction.

BELOW A rocket takes off when the force from the engine pushing it up is greater than the force of gravity pulling it down.

Why do things stop moving?

Things slow down and stop because of an opposing force. One of these forces is friction. Friction happens when tiny bumps on two surfaces rub against each other. Rough surfaces, such as concrete, create more friction than smooth surfaces, such as glass. We use high-friction materials such as rubber on shoe soles to stop people from slipping as they walk.

DID YOU KNOW?
Very fast cars, such as dragsters and rocket cars, need parachutes to slow them down quickly.

LEFT A bicycle's brakes use high-friction rubber to slow the wheels down.

How do parachutes work?

Parachutes slow down a person's fall using "air resistance." Air resistance happens when air molecules in front of a moving object squash together and press back against it. The wide area of an open parachute creates a lot more resistance than a person could create with his or her body alone. This reduces the falling speed of the body.

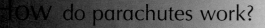

LEFT The wide parachute creates enough air resistance to slow the body's fall.

FORCES IN ACTION

What makes things fall?

Gravity is the force that makes things fall. It is caused by the enormous size of the Earth pulling everything on its surface, or in its atmosphere, toward it. When a stone is dropped in the air, gravity pulls the stone down. Without gravity objects would float in the air.

LEFT A skier is pulled down the hill by the force of gravity.

Why do things float or sink?

Things in water float or sink depending on "buoyancy." Buoyancy is the balance between gravity pulling things down and upthrust. Upthrust is the force of water pushing upward on an object. An aircraft carrier floats because upthrust on its wide hull is greater than the pull of gravity on its great weight.

LEFT Submarines can change their bouyancy to sink or float.

How does a boat's shape help it go faster?

A boat with a sharp, pointed front can go faster than a flat-fronted boat because there is less water resistance. Water resistance is the friction between water and an object moving through it. A boat with a pointed front end allows the water to flow past it easily and smoothly.

DID YOU KNOW?
Maglev trains have no wheels. They move above special tracks using the pushing force of magnetism.

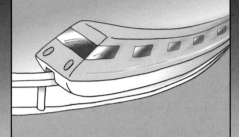

RIGHT Boats with a pointed front, such as this one, are said to be streamlined.

226

LEFT Iron filings spread out in a pattern that shows the forces around a magnet.

How do refrigerator magnets work?

Refrigerator magnets stick to metal because of the force of magnetism, which pulls them onto the refrigerator. Magnetism can be caused by tiny particles called electrons moving from atom to atom in magnetic metals, such as steel. It can also be caused by a force in a magnet's electrons called spin. A fridge magnet is pulled toward, or attracted to, the metal door of the fridge because of the spin in its electrons.

LIGHT AND DARK

Where does light come from?

The Earth's biggest source of light is the Sun. Heat and light energy created by the Sun travels through space in straight lines called rays at almost 187,000 miles per second. The Earth spins around once a day, changing which parts of the globe gets sunlight. This creates day and night. Other things that radiate, or give off, light include electric lightbulbs, candles, and television sets.

ABOVE We make our own light in cities when the Sun goes down at night.

What are shadows?

Shadows happen in places where an object stops light from getting through. Materials that light shines through fully are called transparent. Translucent materials only let a little light through. Opaque materials do not let any light through at all. The shape of a shadow depends on the shape of the object blocking the light. If an object is moved closer to a light source, its shadow gets bigger because it blocks more light rays.

Why do mirrors reflect images?

All surfaces reflect light but, if they are bumpy, the light rays are reflected in all directions. Mirrors are made from very smooth surfaces that reflect the rays back in the same pattern as they hit it, creating a clear image of any object. Words reflected in a mirror appear back to front, as if they were facing away from us and we were looking through the page.

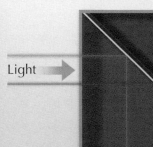

Light

Mirror

Mirror

DID YOU KNOW?
Fireflies flash chemicals that give off light in their bodies to attract mates at night.

How do periscopes work?

Periscopes are devices that use reflecting mirrors in order to see things from a lower level. An angled mirror reflects an image, made up of light, down a tube. A second angled mirror at the bottom of the tube reflects the light again to turn the image back the right way up. Periscopes are often used to see surface ships from underwater submarines, or to see over people's heads in crowds.

ABOVE Periscopes use mirrors to allow people to see things above them.

COLORS

What are the colors in a rainbow?

There are seven colors in a rainbow and they are always in the same order: red, orange, yellow, green, blue, indigo, and violet. Light from the Sun may look white, but it is actually a combination of many colors. When tiny drops of water in the air split white sunlight into its different colors, we see a rainbow.

BELOW A glass prism splits bright sunlight into all the colors of a rainbow.

Why does the sky change color?

Gases and dust in the atmosphere make the different colors in sunlight scatter so the sky changes color. By day, the atmosphere scatters blue light toward Earth so the sky looks blue. At sunset, when sunlight has more atmosphere to travel through before it reaches the surface of the Earth, red light is scattered so the sky looks orangy red.

Which colors do we print with?

People print color images and words on paper using just four colored inks: yellow, cyan (blue), magenta (red), and black. Paper is printed with tiny dots of different amounts of each ink. Our brain cannot distinguish the dots we see separately, but instead, blends them together to make different blocks of different colors.

LEFT You can get new colors by mixing other colors together. For instance, mixing blue and yellow makes green.

How do animals use color?

Some animals have colored skin or fur that is similar to their habitats, so they cannot be seen easily. This is called camouflage. Polar bears are white so they can sneak up on seals to catch, and caterpillars are green to to hide on leaves. Other animals use colors so they can be seen easily and avoided. For example, arrow frogs are brightly colored to warn that they are poisonous.

DID YOU KNOW?
Chameleons change color as their mood varies because blobs of pigment (coloring) under their skin get bigger or smaller.

RIGHT Wasps are brightly colored to warn other animals that they have a nasty sting.

SOUND

What is sound?

Sound is a disturbance of the air made when something, such as a string, vibrates, or moves back and forward quickly. The vibration makes the air move in waves. Our ears detect the moving air and our brains distinguish it as a sound. High sounds, such as notes from a flute, are made by short sound waves. Low sounds, such as a tuba's notes, are made by long ones.

The skin on a drum vibrates when it is banged, producing a sound.

When do sounds get quieter?

Sound vibrations travel away from the thing that makes them. The vibrations spread out in all directions, like the ripples in a pond after you throw in a pebble. The wider the vibrations spread, the smaller they become and the quieter the sound. Big vibrations, on the other hand, make a lot of energy that pushes a lot of air, creating loud sounds.

How do we measure sounds?

Sound is measured in units called decibels. The quietest sounds, such as a leaf falling, are 0–10 decibels. The loudest sounds, such as a rocket launch, are just less than 200 decibels. Noises above 90 decibels are dangerous to listen to because the strong waves of air can damage the sensitive insides of your ears.

DID YOU KNOW?
It is silent in space because there is no air to convert vibrations into sound waves.

RIGHT We can only just hear leaves falling, but an airplane taking off makes a sound that is so loud it can damage our ears.

What are echoes?

Echoes are the repeated noise we hear when sound waves bounce off solid objects, such as a cliff or the inside of a tunnel. If the object is close by, the waves reflect so quickly we cannot hear the echo as a separate sound. Bats use echoes to get around in the dark. They make squeaks and listen to the echoes to work out how far away things are and how big they are.

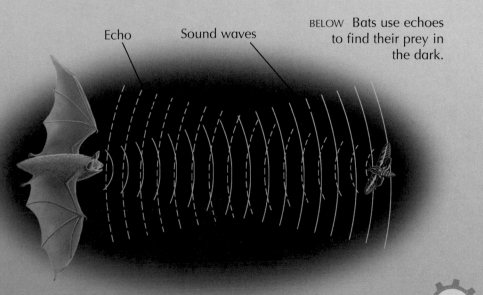

Echo   Sound waves

BELOW Bats use echoes to find their prey in the dark.

HEAT AND TEMPERATURE

Boiling water **212°F** ——

Human body temperature **98.6°F** ——

Room temperature **68°F** ——

Freezing water **32°F** ——

RIGHT A thermometer measures temperature using a liquid that expands as it gets hotter.

What is temperature?

Temperature is a measure of how hot or cold something is. It is usually measured in units called Fahrenheit or Celsius, using a thermometer. Measuring temperature can be vital. For example, living things may get sick when they become too hot or cold. Some substances mixed together change at certain temperatures, for example, heated eggs, milk, and flour cook, forming pancakes!

DID YOU KNOW?
The coldest temperature recorded on Earth was -129°F in Antarctica, and the hottest was 136°F in Libya.

BELOW Liquid metal in steel factories is heated in furnaces to over 1,800°F.

Why do things get hot?

Things get hot because the atoms or molecules inside them are vibrating rapidly. Heat is a form of energy that spreads from hot things to cooler things, until both are at the same temperature. One way things get hotter is by "conduction." This is when the energy of vibration spreads from molecule to molecule, for example, when a spoon gets hot in boiling water.

HOW do coats keep us warm?

Coats keep us warm by trapping air next to our bodies. Air does not conduct heat energy well, so it keeps the heat in. This is called insulation. Other insulators that trap air include double window panes, wool fibers, and down-filled coats. Many animals living in cold places have thick fat or blubber to keep in their body heat.

ABOVE Without winter coats, we would lose too much body heat to the cold air.

BELOW This outdoor swimming pool sits on top of a hot spring.

Why is the water in springs so hot?

The water in a hot spring is much hotter than the air around it because it has been heated by very hot liquid rock called magma. Hot springs are found in places with volcanoes, such as Iceland or Japan. Magma is usually deep underground, but in volcanic areas it can be much closer to the surface. A hot spring may be surrounded by snow but still be as hot as a bath!

201

FREEZING AND MELTING

RIGHT Icebergs float on the sea because ice is less dense (lighter) than water.

does water turn to ice?

Water turns to ice when the temperature drops below 32° Fahrenheit. This is called freezing. When something is cooled, heat energy is taken away from it. That means its particles vibrate less. By the time they freeze, the particles have become closely packed to form a solid. Water is the only liquid that expands (gets bigger) when it freezes.

does ice cream melt?

Ice cream melts and starts dripping when it gets too warm. It changes state from solid to liquid. Changes of state, such as this, are reversible. So, if you put melted ice cream in the freezer, it will freeze and become solid again. The ice cream molecules do not change in taste, but only in the way they are physically arranged.

What happens to puddles on a hot day?

Puddles can disappear on hot days because the water in them evaporates. Evaporation is when a liquid changes to a gas. Evaporation starts when molecules in the water warm up. They start to vibrate and pull away from the other molecules. They spread out until the substance becomes a gas called water vapor.

DID YOU KNOW?
The total amount of water on our planet has remained the same for about 2 billion years!

ABOVE Even on a hot day, some puddles don't disappear completely.

What is the water cycle?

The water cycle is the constant circulation of water between the ground and the sky. Water in oceans, rivers, and lakes is heated by the sun and evaporates. It rises into the sky as water vapor. There, it cools and condenses, that is, changes from a gas to water, in clouds. It then falls to the ground as rain or snow. This water runs into oceans, rivers, and lakes, and the cycle begins again.

203

MATERIALS

Why are saucepans made of metal?

Saucepans are made of metal because most metals heat up quickly. Metal atoms vibrate easily when heated, rapidly passing on the vibrations to atoms around them. This makes metals good conductors (carriers) of heat. Most metals, such as iron, are strong, shiny, hard solids, but metals all have different properties. Aluminum, for example, is light and easily molded.

How is glass made?

Glass is made by heating together sand, ash, and stone in a hot furnace. The molten (liquid) glass is then rolled into sheets, put in a mold, or blown into shapes. It hardens to a transparent solid when it cools. Glass is waterproof and reflects light or lets light through it. It is used to make windows and jars, and also lenses and mirrors.

LEFT The glassmaker dips his blow tube into the molten glass and then blows into it. The glass bulges out and forms a hollow bulb that can be shaped into an object.

What are plastics?

Plastics are artificial materials made by heating chemicals found in petroleum (oil). Plastics have many useful properties. They can be molded into different shapes, they do not break easily when dropped, and they are light and waterproof. There are many different types of plastic. For example, Plexiglass is a tough, transparent plastic and polystyrene is a kind of foam used for insulation (to trap heat).

LEFT Plastic is ideal for making many objects, such as toys, bottles, and chairs.

DID YOU KNOW?
Kevlar is a plastic that is five times stronger than steel. It is used to make light bulletproof armor and ropes to moor enormous ships.

When is plastic a problem?

Plastic is a problem because it does not biodegrade, or break down, as food, paper, or wood do. This means that waste plastic piles up in large holes in the ground or floats around oceans, washing up on beaches. Scientists are developing plastics that break down but can still protect and store goods.

205

ROCKS AND SOILS

What are fire rocks?

Fire rocks are "igneous" rocks. These form when hot molten rock called magma forces its way up from deep underground. Sometimes, it reaches the surface as lava from an erupting volcano, where it cools and hardens into igneous rock, such as basalt. Other times, the rock cools more slowly deep underground to form other types of igneous rock, such as granite.

ABOVE When lava cools, the surface is the first part to turn to rock, giving the lava a rocky "skin."

Can rocks change?

Yes, metamorphic rocks are rocks that have "morphed," or changed. The change was caused by extreme heat and the pressure of rocks around them. If you examine metamorphic rock samples closely, you may see some flattened grains of rock. One of the most common metamorphic rocks is marble, which was originally limestone.

ABOVE Coal changes into diamonds when it is put under huge pressure by rock.

ABOVE Because sedimentary rock is soft, it is easily worn away by the action of wind or water, leaving harder rocks in tall blocks.

Why do some rocks crumble?

Some rocks crumble because they are made of layers of dried mud and sand. These rocks are called sedimentary rocks and include limestone and sandstone. They formed millions of years ago when layers of mud or sand were buried and squashed together underground.

DID YOU KNOW?
Fossils, which are the bones and other remains of ancient animals and plants, are almost always found in sedimentary rocks.

Where does soil come from?

Soil comes from rocks and living things. Wind and water break off tiny rock particles from larger rocks. The particles blow or wash onto land, where they mix with tiny pieces of plants and animals. Other animals, such as worms, mix all the pieces together with water and air as they feed, forming soil.

RIGHT Farmers plow the soil to break it up and make it easier for plants to grow in.

207

FUELS OF THE EARTH

What are fossil fuels?

Fossil fuels are oil, natural gas, and coal, which formed from the fossilized remains of plants and animals. In prehistoric times, dead animals and plants became buried inside sedimentary rocks and slowly turned into fossils. Over millions of years, heat and pressure changed the fossils into fuel, in the form of oil, gas, and coal, which can be burned to release heat.

ABOVE Coal formed from trees that grew in swamps in prehistoric times.

BELOW Oil rigs are platforms in the sea where people drill into the seabed to find oil.

Where do oil and gas come from?

Oil and gas come from rocks deep within the ground. People use very long drills and pipes to release the oil and gas. The rocks are sometimes under land but are often found under the ocean. People drill holes deep into the sea floor and squirt chemicals down the holes to release the fuels. The oil and gas can be made into gasoline, plastic, and other products.

When will fossil fuels run out?

The world's oil and gas will run out by 2050, and coal by 2100, if we continue using them at the same rate as today and don't discover any new stores of them in the ground. Fossil fuels are non-renewable, which means that once they are used up they are gone. To save energy, people must use more renewable energy, such as sunlight, wind, or moving water, that will never run out.

ABOVE Windmills turning in the wind produce renewable energy.

DID YOU KNOW?
The biggest oil tanker is longer than the Eiffel Tower is tall and can carry enough oil to fill over 300 Olympic-sized swimming pools!

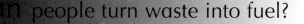

Can people turn waste into fuel?

Yes, heat energy is released when plant waste, such as unwanted wood or crops, is burned. "Biodegradable waste," such as leftover food, animal manure, scrap paper, and weeds, is degraded, or broken down, by bacteria to make biogas and biofuel. Some crops, such as sugar cane and corn, are specially grown to make biofuel.

ABOVE Pig manure can be made into biofuel.

209

ELECTRICITY

What is electricity?

Electricity is a type of energy formed from tiny particles inside atoms called electrons. These electrons can move from one atom to another and this movement is electrical energy. Electricity powers many machines, from flashlights and cell phones to televisions and computers. It moves, or flows, into machines through materials called conductors, which include metal wires.

LEFT Lightning, the streaks or flashes of light that can be seen during a thunderstorm, are sparks of electricity.

Where does electricity come from?

BELOW Some electricity comes from hydroelectric power plants, where moving water turns the turbines.

Electricity is produced in power plants by machines called generators. Fuel, such as coal, is burned in the power plant to turn water into steam. The steam turns a turbine (a set of large circular blades), which rotates magnets inside the generator, producing electricity. The electricity flows through wires to outlets in our homes.

ABOVE Batteries make it possible to use a walkie-talkie without plugging it in.

Why do we need batteries?

Batteries are useful for supplying small amounts of power to portable or mobile machines without the need to plug them into outlets in the wall. Batteries are stores of chemicals that create a flow of electrical energy. Some batteries run out when the chemicals are used up, but rechargeable batteries regain their stored electricity when plugged into the outlet.

DID YOU KNOW?
Solar panels convert light energy directly into electrical energy. They are used in calculators, radios, and satellites.

How do switches work?

Switches work by controlling the flow, or current, of electricity through machines. Electricity can only flow through a circuit, which is a continuous loop of wire. A switch is like a gate that can be opened or closed to break or complete the circuit.

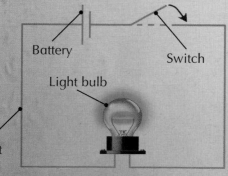

Battery

Switch

Light bulb

Circuit

LEFT A switch turns a light on and off by breaking or completing the flow of electricity through the circuit.

211

MAKING MACHINES WORK

Which machines have motors?

Many machines have electric motors. A motor contains a coil (tightly looped wire) on a shaft in the center of some magnets. When an electric current passes through the coil, the coil becomes magnetized and is repelled by the magnet. This makes the coil rotate and turn the shaft. The turning movement can be used to power machines.

Electric toy train

Drill

ABOVE Many power tools, such as this one used to cut through metal, are driven by motors. Drills and toy trains also contain motors.

Metal filament

RIGHT In an ordinary lightbulb, resistor wires called the filament glow to produce light.

Why do lightbulbs glow?

Some lightbulbs glow because a thin metal wire, called a filament, inside them converts electrical energy into light energy. Other lightbulbs do not use wires, but make light in a different way. Energy-saving lightbulbs have a special fluorescent coating inside gas-filled glass tubes. When a current passes through the gas, it makes the coating glow.

Glass bulb

Metal base that screws into light socket

DID YOU KNOW?
In an ordinary lightbulb, only 10 percent of the energy used produces light. The rest of the energy is wasted as heat.

What makes toasters hot?

Toasters get hot because finely coiled wires make heat to toast bread. These finely coiled wires are called resistors. They slow down the flow of electricity. As the movement of electrons is slowed, some of the electrical energy changes into heat energy. Hair dryers work in a similar way. A fan blows air past hot wires to warm the air up.

LEFT These big loudspeakers are used to make public announcements. Smaller ones are found in radios, televisions, and CD players.

How do loudspeakers work?

Loudspeakers work by turning electricity into sound. A thin cone of cardboard or plastic, called a diaphragm, vibrates when electrical signals are sent through a wire coil. The loudness and pitch (high or low notes) of the sound produced depend on the size and speed of the vibrations.

213

DIGITAL TECHNOLOGY

What is digital technology?

Digital technology includes computers, digital cameras, MP3 players, and cell phones. These record, store, send, and process electronic signals as digital information. "Digital" means that the electrical signals are either "on" ("1") or "off" ("0"). The 1s and 0s form a code that can represent any type of information.

BELOW Many microchips are smaller than a half-inch square.

How do microchips work?

Microchips work using tiny electrical circuits. The circuits are built on paper-thin chips of silicon, a material that is very good at conducting electricity (allowing electricity to pass through it). A single microchip can contain thousands of circuits, allowing it to process lots of digital information. Because of microchips, computers and other digital devices can be small and light.

Where can you use the Internet when you are out?

Laptops can connect to the Internet in most places because they are "wireless." This means they have a special antenna that receives radio signals. The computer converts the signals into web pages or e-mails. Because laptops don't need to be plugged in, people can use them on the move.

BELOW Wireless laptops can connect to the Internet in airports, hotels, and even on the beach.

BELOW Robots, such as this toy, work using digital technology.

Will we have robots in the future?

Perhaps, in the future, many of us will have robots in our homes to do the cleaning and cooking and answer the door. There may even be robot cars that drive themselves along preprogrammed routes. But we are already using robots. For example, in some factories, special robots make the cars and, in some hospital operating rooms, robots even help the surgeons perform delicate surgery.

215

GLOSSARY

Aboriginal
One of the original inhabitants of Australia. Aboriginals were already living there when European settlers arrived.

Asteroid
A small piece of rock in the solar system. Asteroids can vary in size from a grain of dust to more than 600 miles across.

Atmosphere
A layer of gas held around a planet by gravity. The Earth's atmosphere is over 300 miles thick.

Atom
Once thought to be the smallest part of an substance. We now know that atoms are made up of smaller parts known as subatomic particles.

Beak
The jaws of birds, made of bone, which they use for feeding. Also called a bill.

Carnivore
An animal that eats other animals.

Carbohydrate
A substance found in foods, such as sugars, wheat, and rice. Animals eat carbohydrates to obtain energy.

Cell
The tiny unit from which all bodies are made. The smallest animals have just one cell, and the largest have many billions.

Climate
The pattern of weather in an area. All plants and animals are suited to live in their native climate.

Continent
One of the Earth's seven large land areas, which are Asia, Australia, Europe, North America, South America, and Antarctica.

Democracy
A system of government in which the leaders are chosen by people in elections. A government in which the leader is not elected is called a dictatorship.

Desert
An area of land that receives little rain. Because life needs water to survive, fewer plants and animals live in deserts.

Diaphragm
The sheet of muscle underneath the chest that enables us to breathe. It is also used to mean the part of a loudspeaker that vibrates and makes the sound.

Digestion
The process of breaking down food into very small particles. These can then pass into the blood and provide animals with the substances they need to stay healthy.

Digital
A system of storing information using a series of 0s and 1s. Machines, such as computers and cell phones, store this information electronically on microchips.

Echo
The repeated sound that you hear when a sound bounces back off a hard surface such as a cliff or tunnel.

Echolocation
A means of finding objects by making high-pitched sounds or clicks and listening to the echo. Bats and dolphins use echolocation to find food in the dark.

Electricity
The movement of tiny particles called electrons through a substance, such as metal. This causes an electrical current that can be used as a source of power.

Ethnic
A word used to describe the features held in common by a group of people. These can include language, religion, dress, or their country of origin.

Evaporate
To change from a liquid into a gas, for instance, when water turns into steam in a boiling saucepan.

Evolution
The process by which animals and plants adapt and change over many generations. Those that are best suited to their surroundings survive and produce young, while others die out.

Extinction
When a species can no longer survive if it is overhunted or when there is a change in its habitat, for example, when the climate becomes too warm or too cold.

Force
A push or a pull that makes an object speed up or slow down.

Fossil
The body of a dead animal or plant that has been preserved in rock or another substance, often for millions of years.

Galaxy
A group of millions of stars held together by gravity.

Gene
The code within a cell that tells it what kind of cell it should become. In this way, our genes decide how our bodies will look.

Germs
Tiny living things, such as bacteria, that cause diseases in animals and plants.

Gland
A cell or organ in the body. A gland makes chemicals that tell other parts of the body what to do.

Gravity
The force of attraction between any two objects, such as the pull between the Earth and the Moon.

Greenhouse effect
The warming of the Earth due to the presence of the gas carbon dioxide in the atmosphere, which stops heat escaping from the atmosphere. Pollution from burning oil and coal is causing an increase in the greenhouse effect, and the world is heating up.

Habitat
The place where an animal or plant lives.

Hemoglobin

The chemical in the blood that carries oxygen to the body's cells. It turns the blood red when it is full of oxygen.

Herbivore

An animal that only eats plants.

Herd

A large group of hoofed mammals that live together.

Hibernation

A sleep that some animals go into to survive the winter. Their heart rate slows down and the animals appear to be dead.

Ice caps

The thick layers of ice and snow that cover the North and South Poles.

Magma

The molten, or liquid, rock under the surface of the Earth that sometimes rises up through volcanoes.

Molecules

Tiny particles that make up a substance. A molecule can be as small as just two atoms held together by a chemical bond.

Moon

A planet's natural satellite.

Muscle

A part of the body that is able to contract (shorten) and relax (lengthen) to produce movement.

Nerve

A bundle of fibers in the body that carries electrical signals to and from the brain.

Omnivore

An animal that eats plants and animals.

Organ

A part of an animal or plant that performs a particular task. The heart, for example, pumps blood around the body.

Photosynthesis

The process plants use to make chemicals using the Sun's energy. This forms the basis for all other life since it is the only way in nature to take energy from the Sun.

Population

The total number of people or animals living in a particular place.

Predator

An animal that hunts and eats other animals.

Prey

An animal that is hunted by another animal for food.

Puberty

The change that happens when a child's body becomes sexually mature. It usually involves a period of rapid growth.

Rain forest

Dense forest found in areas with high rainfall around the equator.

Renewable energy

A source of energy, such as wind power or solar power, that cannot be used up.

Satellite

Any object that orbits a planet. A satellite is held in orbit by the planet's gravity.

Scavenger

An animal that eats dead plants or animals.

Sediment

Small pieces of rock or soil that settle at the bottom of rivers and oceans.

Senses

The ways we are able to experience the world around us. Humans have five senses: sight, hearing, touch, smell, and taste.

Solar system

The part of space that includes the Sun, the nine planets that circle the Sun, and all the moons and asteroids in between.

Tradition

A way of doing things, such as making music, cooking, or a system of government, that is passed down from one generation to another.

Transparent

The word for any matter, such as glass or water, that lets light pass through it.

Vertebrate

Any animal that has a bony skeleton and a backbone. Animals without a backbone are called invertebrate.

Vitamins

Chemicals that the body needs to stay healthy, which we get through our food.

INDEX

ACKNOWLEDGMENTS

Artwork supplied through the Art Agency by Terry Pastor, Ken Oliver, Peter Ball,
Myke Taylor, Stuart Jackson-Carter, Wayne Ford

Photo credits:
b = bottom, t = top, r = right, l = left, m = middle
Cover: Corbis

1 Dreamstime.com/Pierdelune, 2 NASA, 3l Dreamstime.com/Sebastian Kaulitzki, 3m Dreamstime.com/Thomas Scheiker, 3r Dreamstime.com/Elena Elisseeva, 6 Dreamstime.com/Goce Risteski, 7bl Digital Vision, 7bm NASA, 7br NASA, 8b NASA, 9b Dreamstime.com, 9t NASA, 10t NASA, 10b Joseph Sohm; ChromoSohm Inc./CORBIS, 11t Dreamstime.com/Ken Wood, 12B Dreamstime.com/Goce Risteski, 12-13r NASA, 12tm Digital Vision, 13t NASA, 13b NASA, 14t NASA, 14b NASA, 15t Dreamstime.com/Antonio Petrone, 15b NASA, 16t NASA, 16b NASA, 17t NASA, 17m NASA, 17b NASA, 18t NASA, 19m NASA, 19b NASA, 20-21b NASA, 20m NASA, 21t Dreamstime.com/Johnny Lye, 21m NASA, 22t Amos Nachoum/CORBIS, 22b NASA, 23t NASA, 23b NASA, 24t Dreamstime.com/Steven Bourelle, 24b Dreamstime.com/Daniel Gustavsson, 26b NASA, 26-27m Digital Vision, 27t iStockphoto.com, 27b iStockphoto.com, 28b Dreamstime.com/Jose Fuente, 29t Digial Vision, 29b NASA, 30-31b Dreamstime.com, 30 Digital Vision, 31t Digital Vision, 32b Dreamstime.com/Peter Hazlett, 33b Digital Vision, 34b Digital Vision, 35b NASA, 36 Dreamstime.com, 37bl Dreamstime.com/Anthony J. Hall, 37bm Dreamstime.com/Natalia Bratslavsky, 37br Dreamstime.com/Bob Ainsworth, 38t Dreamstime.com/Ismael Montero, 39t Dreamstime.com/Bob Aimsworth, 39b Dreamstime.com/Tanya Weliky, 40t Dreamstime.com/Natalia Bratslavsky, 41t Dreamstime.com/Asther Lau Choon Siew, 42t Dreamstime.com/Mark Bond, 42m Dreamstime.com/Bob Ainsworth, 46tl Wolfgang Kaehler/CORBIS, 46tr Layne Kennedy/CORBIS, 47t Dreamstime.com/Dannyphoto80, 48t Dreamstime.com/Anthony J.Hall, 49m Dreamstime.com/Tom Mounsey, 50b Dreamstime.com, 58bDreamstime.com/Bob Ainsworth, 68t Corbis, 68bl Dreamstime.com/Stasys Eidiejus, 68br Dreamstime.com, 69tr Dreamstime.com/Christopher Marin, 69br Dreamstime.com/Stephen McSweeny, 69bmt Dreamstime.com/Andre Nantel, 69bml Dreamstime.com/Tim Goodwin, 69bmr Dreamstime.com/Stephen Inglis, 69bmb Dreamstime.com/Dallas Powell Jr, 70t Dreamstime.com/Thomas Scheiker, 70b Dreamstime.com/Jens Mayer, 71t Dreamstime.com/Ian Scott, 71bl Dreamstime.com/Anna Kowalska, 71bm Dreamstime.com/Joe Stone, 71br Digital Vision, 72b Digital Vision, 73t Dreamstime.com/Sergey Anatolievich, 73b Dreamstime.com/Martina Berg, 74t Digital Vision, 74b Digital Vision, 75t Dreamstime.com/Craig Ruaux, 75b Dreamstime.com/Craig Ruaux, 76t Dreamstime.com, 77t Dreamstime.com/Nathan 430, 77b Dreamstime.com/Pomortzeff, 78t Dreamstime.com/Hhakim, 79t Dreamstime.com/Pantoja, 79b Dreamstime.com/Ryszard, 80t Dreamstime.com/Elenthewise, 80m Dreamstime.com, 81t Dreamstime.com/Denis Pepin, 81b Dreamstime.com/Anthony Hathaway, 82t Dreamstime.com/Avner Richard, 82b Dreamstime.com/F2, 83t Dreamstime.com/Carlos Arranz, 83b Corbis, 84t Corbis, 84b Dreamstime.com/Dcrippen, 85t Dreamstime.com/Bernardbreton, 85b Corbis, 86t Dreamstime.com/Alantduffy1970, 86b Dreamstime.com/Janehb, 87b Corbis, 88t Dreamstime.com/Digitalphotonut, 88b Dreamstime.com/Romkaz, 89b Dreamstime.com/Amaritz, 90t Dreamstime.com/Dpw-shane, 90b Dreamstime.com/Matthias Weinrich, 91t Dreamstime.com, 91b Dreamstime.com, 92t Corbis, 92b Dreamstime.com/John Abramo, 94t Dreamstime.com/Vladimir Pomortsev, 94b Digital Vision, 95t Digital Vision, 95b Dreamstime.com/Arturo Limon, 96 Dreamstime.com/Sebastian Kaulitzki, 97bl Dreamstime.com/Daniel Gustavsson, 97bm Dreamstime.com, 97br107b Dreamstime.com/Marzanna Syncerz, 98t Dreamstime.com/Simone van Den Berg, 99t Dreamstime.com/Bruce Shippee, 99bDreamstime.com/Jaimie Duplass, 100t Dreamstime.com/Aliencat, 101t Dreamstime.com, 101m Dreamstime.com/Marek Tihelka, 101b Dreamstime.com/Suzanne Tucker, 102t Dreamstime.com/Aliencat, 103t Dreamstime.com/Rui Vale de Sousa, 103b Dreamstime.com/Vladimir Pomortsev, 104t Dreamstime.com, 105t Dreamstime.com, 105b Dreamstime.com, 107t Dreamstime.com/Eren Göksel, 107b Dreamstime.com/Marzanna Syncerz, 108t Dreamstime.com/Eastwest Imaging, 109t Dreamstime.com/David Davis, 109m Dreamstime.com/Geza Farkas, 110t Dreamstime.com/Asther Lau choon siew, 111t Dreamstime.com/Stephen Coburn, 111b Dreamstime.com/Daniel Gustavsson, 112t Dreamstime.com, 112b Dreamstime.com/Pavel Losevsky, 113t Dreamstime.com/Sebastian Kaulitzki, 113b Dreamstime.com, 114t Dreamstime.com/Simone van den Berg, 114b Dreamstime.com/Monika Wisniewska, 115b Dreamstime.com, 116t Dreamstime.com/Kathleen Melis, 117t Dreamstime.com - Linda Bucklin, 118b Dreamstime.com/Eddie Saab, 119t Dreamstime.com/Mandy Godbehear, 119b Dreamstime.com/Sebastian Kaulitzki, 121r Dreamstime.com, 121b Dreamstime.com/Pavel Losevsky, 122t Dreamstime.com/Ernest Prim, 122b Dreamstime.com, 123t Dreamstime.com/Mandy Godbehar, 123b Dreamstime.com/com Grill, 124t Dreamstime.com/Olga Lyubkina, 125t Dreamstime.com, 125b Dreamstime.com, 126 Dreamstime.com/Cjdabruin, 127br Dreamstime.com/Railpix, 127 bm Dreamstime.com, 127br Dreamstime.com/Has1sue, 128t Dreamstime.com/Pierdelune, 128b Dreamstime.com/Webking, 129t Dreamstime.com, 129bDreamstime.com/Monochrome, 130t Dreamstime.com, 130b Dreamstime.com, 131b Dreamstime.com/Mirafilm, 132b Dreamstime.com/Has1sue, 133b Dreamstime.com/Jenny Solomon, 135t Dreamstime.com/Diomedes66, 136t Tall Tree Ltd, 137t Dreamstime.com/Photodesign, 138l Dreamstime.com/Cjdabruin, 139b Dreamstime.com/Cjdabruin, 140b Tall Tree Ltd, 141t Dreamstime.com/Saffiresblue, 141b Dreamstime.com, 142t Dreamstime.com, 142b Dreamstime.com/Nikonianart, 143 t Dreamstime.com/Amaviael, 144t Dreamstime.com/Lakisf, 144b Dreamstime.com, 146l Dreamstime.com, 147t Dreamstime.com/Rb-studio, 149t Dreamstime.com/Highlanderimages, 149b Dreamstime.com, 150t Dreamstime.com, 150b Dreamstime.com, 151t Dreamstime.com/Webking, 152b Dreamstime.com/Denjoe12, 153t Dreamstime.com/Railpix, 154b Dreamstime.com, 155t Peter Turnley/CORBIS, 156 Dreamstime.com/Dndavis, 157bl Dreamstime.com/Daniel Boiteau, 157bm Dreamstime.com/Elena Elisseeva, 157br Dreamstime.com, 158t Dreamstime.com/Mylightscapes, 158b Dreamstime.com/Elena Elisseeva, 159t Dreamstime.com/ Luisa Fernanda, 160b Dreamstime.com/ Pieter Janssen, 161t Dreamstime.com/Marcus Brown, 161b Dreamstime.com/Vasiliy Koval, 162t Digital Vision, 162b Kim Ludbrook/epa/Corbi, 163t Bettmann/CORBIS, 163b Royal Household handout/epa/Corbis, 164t John Deere, 164b Natalie Fobes/CORBIS, 165l Dreamstime.com/Ilya Pivovarov, 165m Digital Vision, 166t Digital Vision, 166b William Campbell/Sygma/Corbis, 167t Dreamstime.com/Dndavis, 168t Keren Su/CORBIS, 168b Dreamstime.com/Sparky2000, 169t Dreamstime.com/Xiphias, 169b Iain Le Garsmeur/CORBIS, 170t Digital Vision, 170b Dreamstime.com/Kroft, 171t Dreamstime.com/Stougard, 171m NASA, 171b Dreamstime.com/Tsz01, 172t Dreamstime.com - David McKee, 172b Dreamstime.com, 173t Dreamstime.com/Daniel Boiteau, 173b Reuters/CORBIS, 174t Roger Ressmeyer/CORBIS, 174b Dreamstime.com/Zinchik, 175t Dreamstime.com/Edyta Linek, 175b Ajay Verma/Reuters/Corbis, 176b Colin McPherson/Corbis, 177t Dreamstime.com/Craig Ruaux, 177b Dreamstime.com, 178t Dreamstime.com, 178b Jeremy Horner/CORBIS, 179t Dreamstime.com/Bonnie Jacobs, 179b Wendy Stone/CORBIS, 180l Dreamstime.com/David Davis, 180b Matthias Schrader/dpa/Corbis, 181t Dreamstime.com/Kiankhoon, 181b Dreamstime.com, 182t Dreamstime.com/Norman Chan, 182b Olivier Martel/Corbis, 183t Dreamstime.com, 183b Paul Barton/Corbis, 184t Dreamstime.com/Winterling, 184b Dreamstime.com/Pulsartt, 185t Dreamstime.com/Siamimages, 185b Dreamstime.com/Franz Pfuegl, 186 Dreamstime.com/Rafa Irusta, 187bl Digital Vision,187bm Digital Vision, 187br Dreamstime.com, 188r Dreamstime.com/Marcelo Zagal, 188ml Dreamstime.com/Andreus, 189tl Dreamstime.com/Kasia75, 189b Dreamstime.com, 190t Dreamstime.com, 190b NASA, 191t Dreamstime.com/Bigmax, 192t Dreamstime.com, 192b Dreamstime.com/Daniel Gale, 193t Dreamstime.com, 194t Dreamstime.com/Holger Feroudj, 194b Dreamstime.com, 195t Dreamstiem.com/Roy Mattappallil, 196b Digital Vision, 197b Dreamstime.com/Dkye, 198t Dreamstime.com, 198b Dreamstime.com/Jason Stitt, 199t Dreamstime.com/Alan Snelling, 199b Dreamstime.com/Terdonal, 200b Digital Vision, 201t Dreamstime.com/Vasiliy Koval, 201b Dreamstime.com, 202t Dreamstime.com/Pete Favelle, 202b Dreamstime.com/Todd Taulman, 203t Dreamstime.com/Ian Turk, 203b Dreamstime.com/Adeline Yeo Hwee Ching, 204t Dreamstime.com/Martin Green, 204b Dreamstime.com, 205tl Dreamstime.com/Nicole Waring, 205tm Dreamstime.com, 205tr Dreamstime.com/Tomasz Adamczyk, 205b Digital Vision, 206t Digital Vision, 206b Dreamstime.com/Ye Liew, 207t Dreamstime.com/Mary Lane, 207b Dreamstime.com/Elminster, 208t Dreamstime.com, 208b Dreamstime.com/Lancemichaels, 209t Dreamstime.com/Rafa Irusta, 209b Dreamstime.com, 210t Dreamstime.com/Jerry Horn, 210b Dreamstime.com/John Sartin, 211tl Dreamstime.com, 211tr Dreamstime.com/Scott Rothstein, 212tr Dreamstime.com/Attila Huszti, 212tm Dreamstime.com/Adam Borkowski, 212tl Dreamstime.com/Jose Antonio, 213tr Dreamstime.com/Visualfield, 213b Dreamstime.com, 214t Dreamstime.com/Crni_arapin, 214b Dreamstime.com, 215t Dreamstime.com, 215b Dreamstime.com/Andreas Weiss, 216 Dreamstime.com/F2, 218-219 Dreamstime.com